PLEASURES OF LIFE

By a psychiatrist

Dr. C L Ganjoo M.D.

(Many writers and most artists pour out their own life in their work. That makes it realistic and worldly interesting.)

Author

Dr. C. L. Ganjoo, MD.
Ex-senior consultant Sunderlal Jain Hospital,
Formerly medical superintendent, hospital for psych.
Diseases & assistant Professor medical college,
Consultant SMHS Hospital Srinagar, Kashmir.
E-mail: drclganjoo@gmail.com
Ph.: +91-9891427495, +91-8859972522.

ACKNOWLEDGEMENTS

I must, first of all, acknowledge the great encouragement I received for pursuing this work to completion from Dr. S.P. GUPTA M.S. He is a very busy surgeon but more than that a great intellectual and unlike most doctors a man of letters. I cannot but thank him repeatedly, for having gone through the rough format of my manuscript (a tiresome, time consuming job) and to email back the word 'Great' to me. And so this lone word continued to enthuse me all through, especially in my moments of despair when I imagined things going wrong and when a fear of earning disrepute and a label of being a confused person overtook me.

I can never forget my friends—Dr.RM Singhal, MD.Oncologist and Dr.N.Wadhwanim.d. Physician for their loving encouragement and numerous suggestions/corrections which they made in the text.I thank them whole-heartedly for the same.

Dr.Ganjoo.C.L.

CONTENTS

an example, smoking and pollution, alcohol effects, psychological heart attack and panic states.

CHAPTER VIII:

Life-A Love story: in praise of youth, I am a great love bird, beauty of mind, love and love making- a soul elevating experience, sex education for children-a live example.

CHAPTER IX:

Aim of life: psychoanalysis and sex, flower of romance, aim of life, why after-all marry? Usefulness of money, management of long term/terminal illness, summary.

Chapter I

<u>WE DECIDE TO ENJOY</u>

The question is how to make the best of one's time and to enjoy it. In later pages, I have quoted Bertrand Russell the famous British philosopher in favor of the use of Love freely in life to make it sweet and pleasant. He uses the word 'Misfortune' for a circumstance which bars pleasure of love in life and accuses religion first of all for cultivating our morose and miserable mental attitudes.

And this traditional view of life in general is that life has been granted to us, as a golden chance to improve our selves through pious deeds and by remembering our creator the God and to beg forgiveness for our sins. We agree that this theory of life, upon which practically all religion is based, is to say the least, a morbid one and surely the most unfortunate creations of man. As will be said later again, the concept of 'Sin' has been the most malicious of conspiracies hatched against human happiness. We are trying to show that a good and positive life can be lived without caring a bit about 'Afterlife and its heaven and hell (which no one has so far seen)'. It is said that without religion and a fear of

God, ethics and morality in life will vanish and we will behave like animals. This is nonsense. Morality and ethics is a function of our conscience, ordinary reasoning and our circumstances including our childhood upbringing and is not dependent on one's religious beliefs. The old time religion induced guilt into even the children by asking them to seek forgiveness for their sins. Which sins? Even marital love making is declared impious and sinful (read St. Paul). Genital mutilation of girls, amongst a most advanced and rich Muslim community is practiced even in 21st century in order to deprive their women of the sinful pleasures of love. Religion asks people to 'Always remember God, be afraid of him and his wrath and so do the right; all pleasure is sinful'. The new time religion; the scientific religion based on reason says 'Believe in yourself and do the right and be happy at what you can do and achieve'.

Believing in yourself; I assure you, no special effort or so called 'will power' is needed for this. I remind you of a very old and simple prescription of trying to stay happy. Just say to yourself "I want to be happy, I want to be happy, Yes, I want to be happy, come whatever may". Don't laugh at me if I request you to feel if these words repeated three times have made any difference in your feelings. I have tried it on many of my patients and most report immediate benefits, their face changing from its serious contours to one of smiles and even laughter. So if you please, repeat these words often during the day, more importantly if you are feeling stressed by anything anytime. These words said internally to your own self or even loudly in presence of your friends and colleagues will usher in a new atmosphere in and around you and you will really feel happy, as also those around you. Everyone will laugh...You will see that no 'will power' is needed only a mindset, a willingness to be cheerful. Please don't take life seriously; what if you don't own lacs and millions. One does not actually need these to be happy. Happiness is an inside matter!

Before we talk more about this let me also tell you that I ask most of my patients of 'depression' and of low-spirits to try displaying 'An artificial smile' on their face whenever and where ever possible. And it helps. A smile relaxes the muscles of face and head immediately, relieving one's aches in the region and then it relaxes the entire body musculature also. A relaxed body gives a relaxed mind, is an old saying. So whenever you feel your head heavy or aching due to over work, try an artificial smile, even with yourself, all alone. In short laugh it off. You will feel rejuvenated. A relaxed face and an easy smile invariably get the same response from the person you are facing. Smile is infective. Even a grim faced person may melt and give you at least a relaxed-face response. That means he accepts you and that you are presentable and likeable. This is a good feedback and adds to one's self-esteem and self-estimates. That adds to one's confidence which is lacking in most down-spirited and depressed people. Imagine a world where everyone wears a relaxed face and a ready smile, true or artificial. It will be a jolly good place, at no cost. Laughter is a good medicine, is another similar saying. And jokes induce laughter the best and most. A joke is essentially a criticism and condemnation of our societal prohibitions; the more to the point the more mirth inducing. In fact, the most favored jokes are ones that criticize rules and traditions of stifling man's sexual and related pleasures. Man by nature is irked by these prohibitions especially with regard to sexual enjoyment, often dreaming of a 'free society and free life' for himself at least. So what one would himself like to practice and enjoy freely but is not permitted to do by this rigid society he condemns, in a harmless way, through the medium of a joke. He takes his revenge for that unjust prohibition by making others to laugh at this 'cruel' society. By making others laugh at the society he mocks it and in a way challenges it. That is how jokes relieve inner tension. So it is a substitute relief and it works. Creating a joke or even appreciating one is a function of one's intelligence. In fact, Gurudev Tagore is stated to have said that making a good joke is an index of one's intelligence and wit. Dull men can neither create one nor appreciate one. Jokes are also made at other's cost and these also balance a natural hatred in us for those "not ours". In any case these benefit the individual much.

Another side of jokes: Most people have either heard of or seen a man skidding on a banana skin. There are two reactions towards the so fallen down person. The first is of sympathy, so that people around rush to his help and pick him up, enquiring if he has hurt himself. The second reaction is of laughing at him. It induces a sweet and pleasurable laughter in most. Have you ever thought about this? We explain: Sympathy for the fallen man arises because we empathize with him, unconsciously we imagine our own self in a similar predicament and so deserving all sympathy and kind help. The second reaction, almost simultaneous is that this man has proved himself a fool, a gull by carelessly stepping on a slippery peel. And the unconscious mind which has a very high opinion of the self says, "No, I am no fool like him, I am happy that I am so wise. I am very happy that he is a fool and not me. I am very wise, how can I do what he has done? You should have seen how he fell down. Exactly like a circus clown. Eh! but I am very careful every time "Giggles and laughs to himself. "His bottom must still be aching, Fool! They all go like bind men."

Laughs again, rearranging his clothes raising his shirt collar and goes his way. Henh!Wisdom assured!. And nobility. Too.

This was by the way, to draw attention to raw and real human nature. We rejoice at other's misery. Animals basically! Such incidents, however, also help in reducing subconscious tension though vicariously. Comedies that make people laugh fall in this category. Opposite of that is done by tragic shows. They relieve inner weight through abreaction-by helping us to identify with a victim of circumstances. Many are seen weeping during such plays. People feel light and relieved of a weight within after seeing such experiences. We will talk more about such things in pages to come.

It is worth mentioning that the person who starts the first smile or a laugh with a witticism, say breaks the ice, in a group often takes a lead there. He is taken note of. This often benefits.

Back to where we were: Our world is a huge eco-system, balancing and rebalancing itself automatically. Even our little lives and our jobs and work that we do to earn and survive are a part of that system. These little bits are also accounted for and naturally adjusted by this system somehow or the other. If someone loses his job or suffers a loss, what happens then? You think he dies of starvation; No sir. After some troubled time, he perhaps moves to a better work, or at least tries and gets something else to do and survive with. There is a saying that if one door in life closes upon someone, ten doors are already opened for him somewhere else. Only 'man 'himself is impatient and narrow minded. He thinks that this was the end of him and curses himself and his God for his suffering. In time, however, he often realizes that all that happened was for his good only. There are bound to be both ups as well as downs in this long tale of life. In fact, that is what life is made of. So don't lose courage and confidence in yourself, ever. This life is a fun if you realize the truth about it. So read on… please.

Biologically there are accepted and obvious differences between living and nonliving objects, principally the faculties of growth and multiplication through reproduction etc. Power to move is no criterion. A huge railway locomotive huffing and puffing smoke and steam roars it's way on its fixed tracks while a tiny insect feeling the noise and vibration of the onrushing giant feels frightened and for life creeps out from his crevice under that rail line to save himself and goes it's path to a safer place, as he chooses. That is the difference between the living and the nonliving at the psychological/spiritual level. The locomotive has no will of its own; it is bound and guided by the rail track while the little insect has the power to decide its course, action and behavior as he deems proper. Many corollaries follow this statement.

The locomotive cannot but run on its track and that is its destiny, as we may call it. It is destined to go from, say Bombay to Calcutta as is destined for it by an external factor, the railway track. The locomotive has no control over that. But the little insect by virtue of the fact that it can think and make a choice between what is good and what is not good for it has a power in itself which is contrary to the destiny of the giant non-living machine. This is what is called the 'will' power. We can deducefrom this little example that there is nothing which we may call one's 'Destiny' among the living beings. Destiny is for the dead and for the non-living and the word is wrongly applied to living creatures. Life it means is, at the psychological/spiritual level, first of all 'the will to live' and it is this self-will that concerns us here. The average man consciously or otherwise finds life to 'consist of eating and drinking only'. That is also the conclusion to which jokers/comedians, Sir Andrew and Sir Tobby, (in twelfth night) came finally to. But that obviously is not all about our human life. This world is a three dimensional affair <u>but luckily a fourth dimension has been added in case of humans and that</u>

<u>**dimension consists**</u> <u>of our ideas, feelings, experiences and their memories</u>. And that is our life as I understand it. The other three physical dimensions' form just the scaffolding on which real human life (higher mental faculty) rests. Eating and drinking are the fuel and lubrication for our physical body and are no doubt quite pleasurable activities and necessary too. But our mental activities are far more pleasurable and interesting and so to say they add spice and salt to our lives. The average man spends his life very well, no doubt, without worrying or caring to know about many things of his days and nights. The animals also stay carefree as long as their needs of food and drink are met. Human ignorance about 'beyond eating and drinking' can also be a bliss like in animals but the charm of life is different when 'life' is **celebrated** consciously by paying some conscious attention to its whereabouts. And that is human about us and that differentiates us from animals.

The little insect now at some distance after seeing the monstrous engine pass by, feels happy and celebrates his achievement and is thankful to his power of discretion for saving his dear life. Similarly, an active concern about 'where we are, and whence trading' can give a sense of achievement, of safety and above all a sense of direction to our life. In obtaining that sense of direction we perhaps find a purpose and so a meaning for our actions thus far. And in case we do not find our actions serving any purpose, we change our course. This is the use and function of our free will.

Now observing a little further, we find that our insect, who had so intelligently calculated the way to save himself from being massacred by the onrushing engine, suddenly came into the sight of a bird flying there then. The bird swooped down and picked him into his beak to swallow. Was it the 'Destiny' of the insect to be swallowed by that bird? No! Such happenings are the result of 'Calculations and miss-calculations' of life. That is life! If that bird or such like many didn't get their insects to eat they would die of starvation. 'Life lives on life' is an old Sanskrit saying. After a traffic accident involving fatalities, police don't register a case of 'unfortunate destiny' but a case of drunken driving or rash driving or maybe even a motivated murder etc. and attribute the deaths to that cause. But the relatives of the dead go home to inform of the accident adding that so and so was destined or fated to die that way and so it happened. 'God willed it so', everybody agrees. But is that version or that of the police correct?

Hence we decide that the definition and the common usage of the concept of 'Destiny' is mistaken. Deaths in the traffic accident were caused by some miscalculation on the part of the concerned drivers who, we can be sure, must have tried their best to correct their wrong paths and mistakes as far as they could, in those final fractional seconds, before their vehicles did actually collide. We have logically therefore to accept that there was no external agency involved. It was a case of wrong perceptions and calculations on the part of the drivers.

But can't we at least agree that it was in the destiny of our above said bird to eat up the insect and that it was that destiny only that drove the insect to his destined death, out of his nest under the railway line so to be eaten up. Such an acceptance involves unknown factors baseless assumptions, mysterious fore-knowledge of what is to come, and causeless inferences, at more than one point, especially in face of the fact that the insect had planned his safety very intelligently and reasonably. Our theory has to explain the flight of the bird too at exactly that very moment and so on and so involves explaining his destiny too. That will become circular and extended logic and lead to more falsehoods than can be found around such happenings. The matter becomes simpler if we consider another example of a very careful, rule-abiding car driver whose front tire suddenly bursts and the car is thrown into a gorge by the side of the road and he dies. Believers will say that God made the tyre to burst in order to fulfill the driver's destined death then. But has God no other job but to burst other's tyres? He would be better advised to mend burst tyres than destroy them and so prove that he has a constructive mind. Oh God! Am I talking against you? Forgive me, please forgive me! You may burst as many tyres as pleases you; the whole world is yours after all, including all its tyres. You can earn a handsome commission too from tyre manufacturers for increasing their sales. Was I talking 'Atheism'? No sir, I only said what is 'Truism'

Now, what about disease or the deaths because of disease? We are on firmer grounds here. Fate or destiny can here be explained by a combination of 'one's constitution, heredity included, plus one's life circumstances'. If a person is by birth or by whatever he is at a particular moment, predisposed to develop a disease, he will develop that disease if his circumstances also help him in that direction. If a person has diabetes in his heredity/constitution; obesity, lack of exercise and indiscriminate eating will contribute their share and he will develop frank diabetes. Advanced age is, for example a predisposing constitutional risk factor for many diseases like gout, hypertension, cancer etc... So add some facilitating factors to age and one gets these age related disorders. And where is the place of 'Destiny' or any other 'Higher power' in this scheme? In short 'Fate'=one's constitution +life circumstances.

Now talk of 'Will power'! Every one of us has it and that is how we are alive. A person born of diabetic parents has not developed the disease because he has willed to take regular brisk walks, eat sparingly and live a disciplined life. This is a common thing seen every day, nothing great about it. Every one of us exercises some discretion and 'will' to save him perhaps all the time. Even an alcoholic in the throes of intoxication, thinks to himself that he must not drink more than what he already has and then decides to take one more draught or one more glass as the finale of his binge before getting up. Every chronic alcoholic in his heart of hearts wants not to drink any more but surprisingly drinks 'one more' for having reached that great decision. And the cycle continues: Drinking gives repentance which leads to the brave decision of drinking no more, followed by 'Let this be the last'. This final decision lasts unfortunately till the next morning only.

In short, everybody attempts to do the best for himself all the time and that is the 'self-will' we are talking about. This is what sustains life. No supernatural powers or Gods are involved, perhaps.

Do we have an aim? That is an important question! If not, then let us create one and live meaningfully! That has been my effort. Seeking a purpose or some meaning out of life can't be done without knowledge of self as well as the world around, so to say with eyes closed. Do we wake up in morning to just stuff our stomach the whole day and to collect as much money as we can and then go to sleep again to repeat the process the following day and so all our life? Is that alone our life? We are briefly discussing.

Accordingly, please appreciate that the subjects dealt with in this book are mostly not the usual kind like chemistry and biology or even my own psychiatry, for which reference books and guides are available. It mostly describes day/dreams and hopes and aspirations as also the disappointments of a mind, even as it suggests ways of improving one's brain and other organ function while attempting to help find a positive, pleasant, peaceful and a hopeful outline of life. In that sense this is perhaps an unusual and a new work and so liable to mistakes of content as well as of narration. Even when it contains any wrong statements or opinions anywhere or even when its contents present a mixed, at times perhaps some unacceptable view point, may it induce someone else to show us some better, more correct way out. That is the implicit prayer!

Chapter II

<u>ABOUT ADAM and EVE</u>
<u>(In search of happiness)</u>

Looked at for its use or purpose, life is perhaps a meaningless event in the so called 'life span' of any animal. It appears aimless also. We are just born and brought up by somebody without our will or knowledge and then don't know what to do. We continue to live and even strive to live as long as we can. We are encouraged and helped in this by others who are themselves unaware of any reason for so doing. This has been happening since the days of Adam himself. But Adam would have been bored to death had he been alone and so was given a purpose to live, in the person of Eve. And this continues ever since. This naturally brings me to talk of this all important 'Eve-the woman', quickly then.

ABOUT WOMEN Indian tradition has a very interesting mythology about the origin of the first woman in universe. She was to be the ultimate of all beauty and art in the world, a model for anything noble to follow. Accordingly, the Gods put their heavenly architects and sculptors to this difficult work and they in their artistic manner copied the most beautiful things around and putting them together created the female. Wonderful imagination and praiseworthy too! (In later pages, an important role played by a poet too, has been described in this act of creation.) Ancient Greeks would have imagined no less. They were fond of beauty in all things and praised and virtually worshipped it in everything; male body and its beautification received as much attention from them as did the female body. Male sculptures were usually represented naked but female statues in early Greece would be draped. Naked female statues came into fashion after 4th or 5th BCE. Development of body musculature in males received as much attention as did the face and other normally visible features, emphasis being on the whole body depiction rather than on any particular part. So the sense of proportion and aesthetics depicted in art is truly stupendous. A look at the whole work is as breathtaking and overwhelming as a look of its parts separately. Art was considered worship and often Goddess Athena is depicted standing by the side of the artist to help and direct him in his efforts. A male or female statue was considered sacred as well as secular and often depicted ideals like piety honesty, beauty, valour etc. The Hindu imagination did not lag far behind, perhaps overtook theGreek one.

Hindus personified power and beauty of universe in their concept of 'Shakti' the power behind the male Gods that moves the universe. In the concept of 'Prakrati' and 'Pursha' the former manifests itself in the creation and running of this universe in all its diverse forms and changing patterns of boundless beauty. In the concepts of 'Swaraswati' and 'Laxmi' the power of the female is conceptualized as the primary forces that push the creation forward. From whatever sculpted and painted art that escaped the destructive hands of invaders one can realize how feminine beauty has been extolled and praised in early India. Not to speak of attractive and soothing female shapes and figure of the many goddesses even Goddess 'Kali' with her fearful image has also been presented in Indian art as possessing voluptuous breasts and a curvaceous attractive body line. Indians have ever worshiped beauty.

One way of looking at life, here, has been to consider it a sport, perhaps **a divine sport. It is called "Leela", a delightful play, for joy,** for comfort not for misery or repentance over 'sins' never committed. As per tradition, it was on the banks of river Yamuna at Vrindavan that the most illustrated Leela was played long ago but considering that an allegory or an example for others to follow, what is meant is that every heart should become a Vrindhavan, another stage for enacting the Leela of life. And the sweet 'Rasa', the taste, flavor and the joy of life should flow on all sides unhindered by the morose doctrines of sin and repentance.

But before I move to our subject of 'Eve' and her role in life, **a few words about the arts of music and dance** which were highly developed in early India in contrast to Hellenic Greece. Treatment of sound tone, pitch etc. in musical composition is dealt with in very advanced state in 'Sam Veda' and must have needed centuries if not millennia of research and practice before the treatise was actually compiled in writing far later. The same applies to Bharata's 'Natyashyastra' which forms the basis of modern Indian classical dances. There existed numerous schools of thought on both these forms of art but eroticism was not highlighted in most. Emphasis was on self-realization and attainment of peace for the soul through art and little on enjoyment or the erotica. These were most developed in south of India and on the eastern coast. A new strand was added to Indian music by Gurudev Tagore in the form of 'RabindraSangeet'. It has a peculiar depth of its own and can send a person into reveries within moments. Of all the early civilizations, India alone has the place of pride in developing fine arts to enrich human life.

So once again on the 'female': Around the year 1900, Dr. A.A. Brill, the first person to introduce psycho-analysis into America was during a lecture series asked about the changing dress of women. It was a time when traditional loose ankle-long skirts were giving place to pants and shirts among women. And a questioner asked whether males will continue to love women in male attire. Man will love the 'Eternal female' irrespective of what she wears or looks like, was the reply from the famed psychoanalyst. And this stands true! We believe that there lies in the male mind a four-dimensional engram hard wired in the male consciousness for the feminine gender. Three dimensions being easily understood the fourth dimension records the ideal female behavior and her feeling life to complete the picture one loves. The reverse of it being true for the opposite sex. These ideals have been continued and transmitted over thousands of generation with variations attributable to local cultures. One often comes across highly placed men who choose simple, not highly taught and not much yielding to latest fashions, girls as their life partners. Perhaps they are trying to materialize their unconscious dreams. Many men feel a sense of amazement if not shock on suddenly countering an overly painted, thinly and skin-tight dressed female even as she presents an urgent though cheap sex appeal and one wonders if most females really need to go out of the way to enhance their value, if we term it so.

In fact, female dress has come into much abuse lately, tight and less covering dress being indicted as a reason for increase in cases of rape in present times. It makes females look seductive and inviting, is the claim. In fact, there is a thought called the Naked meat hypothesis which supports this idea. It says exposed meat invites vultures. But it may not be so simple. Men are not vultures after all. Many men are incapable of instant erection and forced sex appears brutal. Many remain impotent even after marriage for days in a condition called 'Honey moon impotence'. They can't reconcile themselves to the scene of a naked female; develop anxiety which blocks their erection. Still many people have a subtle idea of sex; its dreamy form called love, which they think has been debased by Americans with their eagerness for quick solutions. Perhaps this philosophic state of love was more prevalent until the modern concepts of societally accepted premarital sex came into news openly and live-in relationships became not uncommon. Is this Americanization of culture, I can't say? Folklore Stories like of Sheerin - Farhad or Laila - Majnoon, are unheard of by newer generations. You meet your love in the forenoon and it culminates in fun in the afternoon and tomorrow you could be with someone else. The naked meat hypothesis is disproved by the sight of semi naked men and women that go about the streets of the entire Europe and America in summer months and on sea beaches without attracting attention of any one practically. Yes, in oriental countries the dress manners being different and especially so in Muslim counties where women are made to cover every inch of their body; sight of a naked woman's legs or other body parts invites ogling and indecent attention. Rape then, it appears is more of an accident depending upon chance or like murder without a reason or dacoity which can befall anyone and so must be avoided in all parts of the world by the possible victims themselves by being more careful, both at home or abroad.

Rapes in reality are no new phenomena unknown to humans previously but cameras and telephones in practically every hand is a new phenomenon and so is the widespread reach of so called 'Media' as a money making business. Rapes used to occur in the past as they occur now and perhaps their frequency in the general population in a given region remains unchanged but their reporting and hyperactive advertisement and at times their politicization has made much difference. The case of 'Nirbhaya' being gang raped and then killed was indeed a brutal crime. It shook the whole nation but our press so exaggerated and presented it that the whole world stood up alarmed and India was designated as the rape capital of the world and all Indians were labeled rapists. One reporter asked the police commissioner of Delhi if he was going to resign his post. Pat came to reply "What nonsense, someone else has committed a crime, why should I resign". Going by that pressman's logic Delhi would need changing police commissioners every morning and evening. Meanwhile some American female film actor who was in Delhi then revealed that she had been raped on gunpoint in New York lately adding that that city was a dangerous place. Further she was frank enough to call her experience as 'Surprise sex'. Please understand the difference in attitudes towards a problem which is common to all everywhere. It should not be criticized too much if a more sober tolerant societal attitude towards a universal human deviation is suggested for Indians also. All over the world the incidence of rapes is almost, almost the same. Then why should Indians hoist themselves up as a nation of rapists and reserve one or two pages in their national dailies for such prosaic, disgusting but sensational news. Murder of the victim in the act makes it gruesome indeed. Yet such beastly tales are not uncommon and that is life; animals that we basically are. Anita Desai a famous novelist in her novel 'fire on the hill side' depicts a rape of a 70 plus bones-in-skin lady social worker followed or proceeded by her murder. Such happenings are not uncommon. If rape was done before she was killed, then it was rape of one's mother and if after being killed the man was obviously a mental patient-a necrophiliac. Such people draw pleasure in biting the lips and cheeks of their dead female.

Involvement of mad people in rapes and crimes in general cannot be underestimated. Many people who are not confident of their sexual prowess try themselves on defenseless children because they fear humiliation at the hands of a grown-up lady if they fail in the act. In certain backward parts of the land many people believe that sex with a virgin, the younger the better, is a panacea for many ailments particularly the venereal disease, which they are otherwise afraid of revealing to others. Children's murder follows often as an attempt to cover up the sex crime.

Going by human history and the study of raw human nature, one may predict that the incidence of rape is perhaps not going to decrease overtime with the remedial measures proposed by our press and the media. They have so primed the general public to this reporting of rapes that every single rape news sends shivers down the spine of people and they demand banishment of rape from fundamental human behavior itself, with immediate effect. So, what can any government do to satisfy the public demand but bring in laws to murder the culprits. Since the ordinance for hanging of rapists was promulgated many, many have already been reported and one can be sure a 20-fold more must have gone unreported. Advocacy of harsher/capital punishment for rape has apparently boomeranged and rape is lately followed by rapists burning the woman in order to destroy the proof of their crime. And gang rapes seem to be a function of intolerably increased density of population in this blessed country where Goons also don't walk the street singly but in gangs and cohorts and so commit a crime together whenever and wherever chance permits. Thinly populated countries don't report gang rapes as frequently if at all, Sexual instinct is a very strong power in life and those who know about evolution of human society will remember how and why even the primitive forefather was murdered by his sons because he had usurped all the females of the herd denying the sons any share in them.

Burning and killing after rape: From a psychoanalytic point it may be interesting to speculate why women's organizations have become more vociferous after the reports of burning of rape victims have increased. Recently a prominent office bearer of one lady's organization, herself a young beautiful lady went on prolonged hunger strike, exposing herself to grievous peril, demanding a summary trial at it's lengthiest of 21 days only for culprits. Naturally any scientific and inquisitive mind will ask **why she did not undertake and show a similar bravado and eye-catching reflex earlier**. Have rapes (frankly termed surprise sex by the above noted American actress) grown dangerous and bitter, after being tolerated/accepted and hushed up for millennia? Further questioning in the matter may reveal raw human desires working on both sides of the gender divide with equal intensity and the results astounding! This **un**conscious human mind un/fortunately never keeps quiet; only seeking pleasure for itself all the time, the conscious civilized mind notwithstanding. When ladies were not burned or tortured after rape like Nirbhaya the irrepressible **un**conscious would exclaim "If that lady could be chosen for "Surprise sex" why not me? I am no less attractive and am young and dashing too, this is patently unjust. Wouldn't Greek God Zeus rape goddesses of his liking? He never harmed them; never mutilated or burnt them. Accordingly no goddess ever complained against him nor lodged a police report.After all what is wrong with civilized and gentle rape? It can be a good change, a curiosity satisfied, and a pleasant 'surprise'. Quick would come a rap from the civilized **conscious** mind, "You rogue, why can't you be quiet for a moment?You think I don't need to enjoy life but why can't you see the web of morality woven by these males around us- the females only?Themselves theyare free to do whatever and where-ever they enjoy. This man's world runs on pretentions.And we are forced to abide. Don't you know how religious, god fearing and conforming I am? And don't you care for the image of high character and of an innocent woman that I have built over the years? And don't you see how respectful I stand in society's eyes? This well publicized hunger strike will earn me and the entire women folk still; higher respect and honors', I am shocked at your wickedness and negligence of facts of actual life!" And this mental debate between the **conscious** and the **unconscious** minds goes on and on unknown to the lady herself resulting in an ambivalent and silent but inquisitive response to the news of rape in the neighborhood. But now in the changed scenario of burning after the act, both the minds concur that "surprise sex" has grown frightful and dangerous. Now they cooperate, resulting in hunger strikes and general anger and rage. Now they both want Revenge. Revenge, yes, yes. Rapists must be hanged, both shout in unison. **But the unconscious mind quietly quips:** Not the gentle ones please!

Ah this psychoanalysis! This science of the mischievous, digging up fossils?

The above is stated neither for jest nor for amusement of the reader but to repeat, given the real nature of life forces that **it is impossible to stop rapes and for that matter any other crime from happening**. These happen without any forewarning and advance intimation. They are of the nature of accidents and can befall any one any time. The best one can say about these is to be cautious yourself and try to avoid risky situations. There neither is or was nor ever be any dearth of criminal elements on earth. This remind us that we are after-all animals only, carrying a thin veneer of civilization for convenience and deception. Morality, piety and religiosity etc. are but handy tools.

Lately, a movement named **"Me too"** has **also** got started by women themselves to shame and even get their assailants punished. It is perhaps a good move which may add to their self-confidence.

It may be interesting however, to know a psychoanalytic explanation for this female behavior-a cry which is raised in most cases after a lapse of years: A lady hears or comes to know that her former assailant/paramour has victimized some other lady/s also. This gives her "courage" to vent out her own grievance too; the time being ripe to strike. True, very true!

 In its attempt to explain human behavior in rational terms, analysis finds and interprets her pious "courage" as her 'jealousy 'for those other women who induced/seduced her man. The fire of jealousy burns more acutely at finding that the man has chosen some other women in preference to her. She feels humiliated. Her very womanhood and her essence as an attractive satisfying lady have been questioned. She had up till then lived her life calmly and peacefully, having buried all 'bad' memories deep into the past until the disturbing news reached her, setting her aflame. The only way to extinguish the fire of hatred appears to go to the press and thereby to assure everyone and above all her own conscience about her own piety and good character and her excellence as a female, as the others have now done. Sensible, very sensible!

The unconscious reasoning within her goes like this: God forbid, I am not an ill charactered person. Nobody can blame me. But he perhaps could not stop himself then; I looked terrific, really dashing. Perhaps he could not; yes, yes, he could not stop himself because of that and that is why I kept quiet about it. I also feared public shame then. Above all I am a God-fearing person. But I can very well imagine those wicked ladies. One or two look ugly in the press photographs- bitches. No comparison with me. I still look young and attractive. How could he agree to do it with them, I am aghast! Horrible looking monsters; they must have tricked him into the act; woe befall them. But I am shocked, how he could stand them? -all garbage! I am not jealous of those fallen women; on the other hand, I have all sympathy for them. Yes, yes, I am not jealous of them; after all I am so reasonable and noble. How can I be that bad? But the present evidence and the entire story shows prima facie that he is mean and rapacious and has perhaps exploited these ladies also. Then he is a true devil. Had I known that he is such a serpent, you think I would keep quiet this long.I would have raised hell and heaven against him. Iwas too simple and inexperienced; just in my salet (Salad) days then. And someone comes and cheats you then; ooph! Sin of the gravest kind! God save my soul! I was ever a charactered person. It is he who cheated me because of my innocence. O.K, I was very attractive, but was that my fault, after all. But who knows about those ladies, how good they are? If they knew this serpent, how did they fall for him then? They ought to have judged for themselves.They can't go without blame, eh. Yes, they do deserve much blame. It takes two to rub. Mischievous women; blaming others! I hate such people. I feel suffocated by these dramatics.I was so peaceful up till now! But what business had they with him? Promotion? Wanted a job or some contract perhaps? But that is done across the table, not sitting close by and hugging each other or lying in bed to discuss. Why didn't these pious ladies protest there and then? Oh! I am worried about their gossip.I was never involved in their dirty ways. In any case it is never late; let me also go to the press to set right my history (lest it be leaked between them) and restore the peace of my mind/conscience. We must expose that devil, this eternal sinner.

We said above that this 'Me too' movement may prove a good thing in time but going by well laid statistics a huge percentage of females are subjected to one or the other kind of sexual assault some time in their lives. Worse still the traditional image of females being a harmless gender is being challenged by revelation of forced rape of males to the extent of 4-7%. So can one expect all those affected females and also the males to gather 'courage' and rise up in 'me too' some day? What will be the shape or mis-shape of society thereby wherein most males and many females (nice uncles, sweet aunties loveful cousins including) may be 'shamed' by the 'Me too- ers'.

Before we move on, a few words about our mental working: Someone may say that the above kind of reasoning could be taking long to decide things in a person's mind. No! In the unconscious mind many related topics are processed simultaneously and almost instantaneously.Cut, copy, compare with old memory, distort, delay, deny, weld, paste etc. and above all; 'pleasure for self and interests of self'; all is done at sub-atomic velocities and finally the decision is forced on the conscious mind. **Forgetting** unpalatable memories is its work and so are unexplained remembrances, mistakes and attitudes in life etc. Delay in thinking and decision-making is in the working of the conscious mind; of course, forced on it by the unconscious often times. And all this unknown to the individual; that is the miracle of our unconscious.

The me-too lady referred to above can swear that she never felt bad about the other ladies and it is agreed that she is right in her own way, because the subject she is dealing with is too emotional and hence dealt with at her unconscious level. She knows nothing about why she is reacting the way she does. She is honest about her feelings. If confronted she will declare: Oh my god, what blasphemy, I am a god-fearing person, why should I be jealous of those ladies whom I don't even know? Those ghastly looking creatures! Even now I can't reconcile to what they report. After all, how could that man fall so low? No, no, he must be punished, that Satan (shaitan), that satyr (mythological Creature with a human face but a horse below the navel and hence capable of unlimited and indiscriminate mating). But women have gone wanton these days. At the slightest hint they lie down before any tom dick and harry, these sinful fallen women! Eh! But he must be exposed and punished, that serpent! I didn't know, that is my sorrow! God forgive me! But he can't be let off, oh those ghastly women! Oh, I remember my greener days; I was truly irresistible, and it was not entirely his fault then. But these damned bitches! No, no, he must be exposed! I feel dishonored and let down. How did he fall that low? And why after all should I speak untruth? I am a god-fearing person and I never lie, after all what have I to conceal?

These days' scientists are attempting to create artificial intelligence. A robot which brings forth a cup of tea for his master from the kitchen and on seeing further guests pouring in, himself goes again to the kitchen to bring as many cups more as are the guests. Again, after identifying an enemy he shoots him down by himself. These are indeed marvels and we call them artificial intelligence. Just think, these are only mechanical and electronic sleights not true intelligence. Human intelligence is not just a problem-solving mechanical process but more importantly a means of adaptation to one's environment and the faculty of mastering that environment. It is not as simple as just handing over a cup of tea to your guest, but it is 'how' you hand that over and much more also. The emotions and sentiments that accompany and are simultaneously expressed while handling the tea cup for your guest, your spouse, your father, your child etc. are different for each occasion and determine the value of your cup of tea as well as quality of your efforts at building relations around, for a successful social life.

As said, Human intelligence is not merely a calculating, thinking and limb muscles activating mechanism but more importantly a process of feeling and of being perceived as feeling for others around. This feeling consists of perceived emotions, sentiments and 'affects' in a situation. Above we talked of subatomic speed of unconscious thoughts- almost an instantaneous processing. This super-speed is possible there because the unconscious does not think in lengthy 'Ideas' but in brief, to the point emotions and affects mostly. Logic and calculation are absent in unconscious thinking. Its guiding mantra is only pleasure and interests of the self, to be taken care of. Affect (Sentiment) behind an idea is transmitted to it and there it evokes a hundred similar sympathetic as well as a thousand opposing counter-affects. These act and react on each other mixing like differently colored vapors', or like small little charges(forces) shooting at each other. A quick resolution takes place and is immediately transmitted back to consciousness but now it stands modified in a hundred ways. It has been 'colored' so to say in the color of the individual unconscious. Sudden unexpected, inopportune, unthought about, bursts of anger or even of affection and love in response to routine stimuli or events in an otherwise balanced person, attest to the high velocity illogical processing of thought in the unconscious. Then we say that the response was caused by his 'complex'. This, our feeling or affective life is our actual and real life, and this is what differentiates ours from the life of a beast. When you on a formal occasion offer a cup of tea to a distant relative who is fighting a court case against you and when you offer a cup of tea to a beloved person of yours, the externalities of events may look alike but the intrinsics are different. This is not possible for an 'artificially intelligent' robot to achieve now. A Freudian slip (you forget to add sugar to the guest's cup) for example may occur; your smile is strained, warmth in dialogue is lacking, you are tired of his presence soon etc. All these happen under the effect and as a result of your 'feeling life within you'. And this completes our 'intelligence' and makes it 'human'. Our robot has still to go miles to catch up.

ROMANCE; Now, going from the theoretical to the practical side of the story of 'Eve' and her love and since this is intended to be some description of my life, I must confide that I have been a great love bird. I remember GurudevRabindernath Tagore writing that a life of love gives one a wild blossom of multicolored glorious flowers and later an autumn of sweet and delicious memories. Great minds, great glorious flowers and still greater delicious memories! I am sure Gurudev must have poured his personal experience out. I hereby attest to this great man's statement. I have ever been a worshipper of beauty, beauty in all it's shapes. And if I declare that the most beautiful creation of nature is a beautiful lady I may be contradicted. If lions could write books and make speeches some great lion would immediately pounce upon me roaring scorn and contempt for having belittled his beloved she-lion. More about it later.

PSYCHOANALYSIS; It is said that beauty lies in the eye of the beholder. Yes, perhaps we have engrams of our ideals etched in our subconscious and much depends upon how and how much the external cues match with them. If for example an object appears beautiful and attractive to us, it is so because we perhaps already have an engram of that object, or may be of some of its components that are already represented in our mind and even identified with either gender in some way closely or distantly. These had appeared pleasing and satisfying to us some time now or even in earlier human evolution at large to leave a permanent pleasant association of itself in our psyche. Our mental world is essentially a world of associations only. Our memory, intellectual function, recognition, recall, calculation and most importantly our feeling life is dependent on the existence of a robust system of associations within us. Neurobiologists hypothesize that these associations are physically based in millions of neurochemical connections within our brain, but this is too subtle and premature to demonstrate as yet. In any case, psychoanalysis gives our associations the importance these deserve. Free association is a simple technique to help an individual remember even long forgotten events. I will give a simple example; suppose you have forgotten your car keys somewhere and while leaving in hurry for office the next day you don't find them at their usual place. Instead of rousing the whole house to search the keys, you simply stand calmly at one place and try to recall the chain of events of the previous evening. You will say to yourself 'after I locked the car yesterday evening I went to my daughter's room, gave her the painting box she had demanded, and I remember having the keys in my left hand that time. Then I went again to the garage to collect my forgotten lunch box from the car, closed and locked it's door and then threw a soiled cloth collected from the car into the dust bin in the corridor and yes, I did hear a metallic sound accompanying the fall of that cloth then but didn't give any importance to that because I was feeling tired and wanted to reach the bed room quickly. Now you will suddenly rush to the waste basket in the corridor to search your keys and lo, you have got them. Such experiences come one's way often, but we don't give much weight to them. But Freud did, and invented his method of Free associations to recall even long forgotten experiences this simple way. I hope, the scientific and the common-sense basis of free association technique are amply borne out by the above example of lost car keys.

There is a more interesting side to it and that is the 'Why 'of it. Why did you forget your keys then on that particular evening and not ever before? The answer to this 'why' often leads us to the cause of a psychic act or illness and this in combination with analysis and interpretation of dreams is 'psychoanalysis'. It has at many places in literature been noted that so and so lost their marriage engagement ring somehow. Well the 'Why' or the cause of that forgetting of the ring comes before us when we know that the marriage has soon thereafter floundered. Separation was wished for by one of the partners and loss of the ring only gave an advance intimation of it, as translated psychoanalytically. This is how analytic interpretation proceeds.

We are all bisexual in our making both in physical as well as in psychic lives that means there is a shadow government working within us every time, in case of males the shadow is female and vice versa, which ever sexual component predominates according to our gene make up, determines our finished exterior product whether we look and behave as becomes a female or male. The non-predominant sex nonetheless, functions unknown to us and determines our same sex and even the opposite sex likes and dislikes. What is said here is perhaps too simplistic. Anyway, whatever be the cause, I love, intensely love what is commonly called 'Natural' around us. I for example, am bewitched on seeing an ordinary little thatched village hut situated in solitary circumstances near a forest with all the nearby greenery and verdure at it's command. The person who owns that, I call a real king and would gladly exchange places with him. Just imagine such a setting, with no electric lights and no chitter chatter of society! Peace reigns supreme here while the murmur from a stream flowing nearby reinforces the silence that has already held you in it's soothing lap and if one be lucky to be there on a full moon night; o you have earned millions! It is an experience you will never forget. I have tried my utmost to create my little world amidst such circumstances but demands of livelihood come in between me and the demands of my ideal. I am a lover of animals too and attempted rearing cows one time in my life. My two cows and myself had an extremely close relationship. They and their calves would play with me, kiss me and lick me in my face and head and I in turn would kiss them on their snouts to our mutual satisfaction. And this brings me to **a rare encounter** that may interest you too:

One late evening while returning home to Shyamkhet, Nainital in Uttarakhand I encountered a wild animal (am loath to call him an animal but can't find a better word, perhaps a 'spirit' or 'angel' would be apt), a rare rapturous beauty on the Ramgarh road. I was in my car and I saw it immediately as I turned a corner, his eyes glittering in the light of my car. My surprise and joy knew no bounds and I slowed down at once to reach him that stood silent on the left bern of the road as if waiting to board the next bus to Bhowali. As we neared, he looked patiently on to the front of my car while my eyes stayed fixed on his magnificent round looking cattish face with whiskers. He didn't move and so I slowly reached near him-by his side. It was no distance from the left-hand window of the car and I was ecstatic, having a full view of my neighbor and I suddenly realized that the glass pane of that side was full open, my right side being closed. Somehow it made no difference to me, daredevilry I believe or just, just a careless moment of pure bliss, so much surprise. He turned his calm countenance towards me and I had a near view of his wet snout, and his innocent looking face; nothing but three feet of cool jungle air intervening between we two. He was looking thoughtfully at me and I can't say what I thought in my mind then. It was a moment of trance for me! How could I have thought anything? It was a vision; a revelation, the like of which I could never have even dreamt. My feelings perhaps were a mix of joy and surprise; surprise at how, how such a thing could materialize in my front without my seeking it. There was no sense of fear or strangeness in me and I think there was reciprocity of that affection between us. Reminded of the snouts of my cows and their progeny I strongly yearned to kiss that dear snout too. He looked peacefully at me, into the interior of my vehicle and I watching him with loveful eyes and perhaps a twitching mouth-twitching for a sweet kiss on his snout, for near a minute or more, may have been two or more minutes. I would have loved to ask him what he was thinking then or at least what he was thinking of me because he looked thoughtful, deeply so. I wish that were possible! And then, but soon, very calmly he turned his head right and took a slow-film leap down from the road and I was left alone gazing at his upturned tail waving me a good bye. His tail appeared very long to me- almost the full length of my car and it was very powerful also. I stood bewitched and mesmerized in that silent jungle wilderness not able to comprehend what had happened; this sudden occurrence-unsought, as it appeared to me then. A vision, an epiphany! Now regaining my senses, a little, I felt joyous, limitlessly joyous; I remember the after effect well. A cosmic force had materialized in skin tight dress of shiny white with dark brown spots looking exactly like a leopard as we see them on pictures, for a brief moment for me to see and appreciate its beauty and magnificence. I did not, perhaps, could not move my foot from the brake pedal to accelerator for quite some time; I was immobile-just naturally immobile. I was spellbound, totally relaxed in body but wonder struck! Was it my great luck? I can't disbelieve.

A sorrow, a faint sorrow, however, lingers in my heart ever since: we did not say those formal words 'good-bye' to each other! Or even shake our hands before parting. We forgot to fix the venue and time for our next meeting. It was perhaps because I was, as I said in a hypnotic daze and he in puzzlement at meeting a peaceful so called 'human'. He could have been suspicious too, lest there be a trap. But he must also have seen genuine joy in my face and my eyes and got filled with wonder how humans had turned meek and loveful. It is my belief, had we fixed our next meeting and then next and then again and again a new next, I would have declared myself the luckiest and the happiest man on earth. Day- dreaming? That unrecognized infinite source of pleasure of man's life. Common man's luxury!

A prince from the kingdom of mighty Himalayas had visited us, -their ambassador of peace (Shanti-Doot), it dawned on me. He was right royal, civilized and too humane. He took away my heart! His silent message: 'live and let live; we love you.'

Such encounters with wild life must be not unknown to villagers around but the effect it had on me was, I think, quite uncommon. It changed my perception of life; it was a dear, a very dear, occasion in my life.

Again Sirs, note how my mental associations of the wet snout worked without my willing it and I was moved to an emotion of love instead of a sense of fear, for an unknown fearsome animal.

Psychoanalysis as a theory of human conduct is like a religion compelling and it' practice full of delights. Once you understand it, its logical formulation and explanations of behavior become manifest and one comes to believe it. Need for quick results in therapy with changed times have put it in the background but I consider that while seeking ends one must not forget the means to those ends. Psychiatrists these days go by the biochemical theories of psychic disorders and accordingly treat them quickly with modern drugs by altering the neurochemical pattern of brain without understanding the intermediate psychological working behind the disorder. How do our mental defense mechanisms come to play their part in our normal as well as abnormal talk and behavior? What would our life have been without these; how dull and uninteresting. To illustrate it I give a small Freudian joke described by a famous psychoanalyst for a change as well to illustrate how our mental mechanisms work: An elderly man was trying hard to please a young woman by all means at his disposal. One day he presented her a very costly necklace. The lady after thanking him replied 'Mr. John, you may not benefit by spending so much money on me because my heart is already given away'. John replied 'Darling, I have never aspired as high as that'. See how an outright sexual remark has been converted into a sublime civilized reply without offending anyone but still meaning what it actually wanted to say openly. (His aspiration concerned only her lower body parts; he had no use for her heart etc.) How has the medical world forgotten the value of "Freudian slips of tongue, the meaningful mistakes of pen, the above shown sculpted language of civilization" etc.

Three and a half Jews, I would say deserve credit and our salutations for having changed the thinking of our world for all time to come; Karl Marx, Freud, Einstein and Lenin. Lenin was a half Jew by heredity, from his mother's side; he showed the way to human happiness through practical scientific means. Another name for Marxism was 'Scientific materialism' (in contrast to 'grocer's-village bania economy i.e; our capitalism') and Lenin implemented it in Russia. He however died on Jan. 1924 and Stalin took up the task. Historically Russian revolution took place in October 1917 but as a matter of fact the revolution was a long continuing process and truly revolutionized the entire history of mankind. Its lessons,far more important and meaningful than that of French revolution, will never be forgotten. On 4th October 1957 exactly forty years from the famed October revolution the Soviet Union sent up into space the first ever artificial satellite to revolve round earth, from its launching station in Bikanur in Kazakhstan. The same Backward and primitive Kazakhstan and Azerbaijan in central Asia where people had never seen a leather or a rubber shoe and went about in footwear made of dried hay (Paddy grass) or simply bare footed. Now just after 40 years these areas including far off frozen Siberia were turning out scientists, doctors and engineers to serve their space stations, man their hospitals and factories. Russia overtook 200-year-old America in aero and missile technology etc. in 70 years.

Greatest achievements of Soviets were in improving the common man's lot. Within these 70 years everyone had a house to live in, everyone was assured of his job and everyone had been educated enough to call himself literate besides the streams of scientists, doctors, engineers and their like that flowed out. Crime and criminals were greatly checked. One authentic source reported calculable reduction in mental diseases. That of course is on expected lines because life under assured conditions must become easy and tension-free. Devil of greed and religious intolerance was under control! And this fact is important and noteworthy for us in our search for human happiness.

And where are we at the end of our 70 years of independence? And has America eliminated it's poverty, joblessness and houselessness even after it's two centuries plus of effort? Yet the rich people of the western world lost sleep merely on hearing the name of communism. It threatened their riches and wealth obtained through capitalist cut throat competitive business of fraud and imperialist exploitation. The words 'communism' and 'socialism' did to capitalists, what the proverbial red rag does to the raging bull. All the major powers attacked that nascent state of the people and forced it to violently curb all opposition that was incited against it by these enemies. This violent reaction of the Russian state against its fifth columnists (white armies) who were actively supported by the capitalist mafia gained for it the notoriety of committing genocide and for communism as a doctrine of being not compatible with peaceful implementation. Give a dog a bad name and then hang it, is an old useful saying. Accordingly, communist Russia was opposed tooth and nail, vilified and ultimately destroyed clandestinely, the last nail in its coffin being that driven by Mr. Gorbachov who was perhaps a CIA mole implanted in the system for that purpose. What Reagan and Thatcher could never have achieved through cold war tactics, Gorbachov did for them through internal sabotage. He received a Nobel Prize for the services rendered in addition to untold pecuniary benefits. Demise of communist Russia is a sad human tale to tell! It was the first scientifically planned experiment in egalitarianism and equality for humans, with humaneness as its guiding principle but for the capitalist mafia, who considered greed a better motive for progress. Whose progress?

Sorry for this diversion, but it must now be said that Freudian Psychoanalytic theories also have been neglected to the point of their death because huge multinational pharmaceuticals wouldn't stand anything to stand against their profits. Short lasting symptomatic treatment with drugs produced by them, has come into vogue. Why should psychiatrists bother about the hidden psychic cause of diseases? That needs hard study! Since we are discussing human happiness, it must be noted that economic and social equality as was introduced in Soviet Russia, did prove a great help in improving the happiness index of the population. In contrast, depression and other disturbed mental states are commoner and increasing by the day in competitive capitalist states.

After world war II some renowned intellectuals were advocating a one-world government with the aim of ensuring a lasting peace and of eliminating wasteful expenditure on armies and armaments. That same money would be used to eliminate poverty, they said. They would not know that world would go into even smaller bits fighting for petrol and to spread the message of Allah. Suicide bombers and terrorist gun men were not born then. Similarly, during mid-twentieth century many great men were upbeat with the advent of computers predicting that life will become easier with drudgery eliminated and competition reduced among working men. Their working hours would be reduced by the use of automation and plenty of time would be available to humans for recreation and enjoyment. Bertrand Russell among others predicted slouch a pleasurable future for us. Himself a known educationist, Russell recommended a four-hour duty period for teachers in particular. Accordingly, many people had started dreaming of an easy and a happier life pattern in times to come. Alas these have proven just fond hopes only. With capitalism going strong, the lure of money on the one hand and religion getting more bigoted and fundamentalist on the other life has become more complicated and tense. Thirst for more earnings coupled with urge to spend more in order to be and to look more prosperous has taken hold of man. Workers in large companies working on the same 'Ease generating computers' that Russell dreamt of, in our mega-cities, start their day around dawn to be freed only in the dark hours of night. When the tired husband reaches home his wife and children are already asleep because they in their turn also have to start their next anxiety filled day equally early. That is the way; the family' has gone: each member worried and anxious in his own way. The computer-master-husband is all along tormented for improving his work-output and it's quality by the ubiquitous 'manager'. Shareholders of his company are awaiting better dividends! Consumerist advertisements and temptations of an 'Ideal and luxurious 'life as lived by the next door neighbor and other comparable relatives haunt every mind. Alas! there is peace neither at home nor at work. Mental illness especially depression and anxiety states are rampant and increasing by the day. The devil is at play! Free.

II a. (A NOTE)

Before we proceed any further I must remind the reader that the only places where a person may undress and get naked with impunity, are his bathroom and his doctor's clinic.Better or worse still, is a psychiatrist's clinic and his couch, where he completely undresses his mind to reveal his innermost desires, wishes, his fears and phobias and his secret life as a whole.(Is hamam main sub nangeyhotehain 'everybody is naked in this bath' and strangely the same equipment and working Methods-Ideas and ambitions are found in all, sage as well as the savage).Undressing in a bath room, many must have realized, is felt as a relief; a freedom from one knows not what.It is a pleasurable feeling if you remember. This pleasuresomeness in nakedness is an analytic tale which cannot be talked of here. Nevertheless, the reader should give it a thought. It will amuse!

In the succeeding pages plenty of digressions into the domains of economics, politics, religion, history, children's sex etc. have been made. These are what comprises sociology: a scientific objective study of societal thought and behavior that affects and greatly determines individual mental welfare and pleasure or it'sobverse. In effect then this is a socio-psycho-medical study taken up in our attempt to describe a meaningful life.

Above we have referred to a conspiracy of 'sin 'against human happiness. This is a mental conspiracy. Similarly, we have social and community and group conspiracies unleashed by vested interests to keep us in turmoil every time. These can be bracketed under the term 'Disruptive politics' which can have dire results. While we innocently seek mental peace and pleasure for the individual, there are diabolical influences around seeking to disturb that peace not only of the individual but of the entire community and the country. Knowing these destructive currants is the first function of any conscious mind. After all isn't it futile to seek individual peace, happiness and salvation when the entire surroundings are in turmoil or are sought to be set into turmoil. Seeking individual peace through counting beads, sitting in a dark corner, can give a false sense of peace, obtained through autohypnosis and ignorance. Should that ostrich's peace be our goal in life? So don't please dismiss that knowledge of prevailing circumstances and times as 'Cheap politics'. This is sociology.

It is not very far-fetched,for example, to talk of individuals called 'progressive intellectuals. All it needs is a tender heart with a fertile imagination and a zest for publicity to be called an intellectual these days. Funds are no problem; enemy agents are ready sponsors. These intellectuals are very good people basically; so good that if they see a dacoit they believe that he has been tormented by this cruel society so that he feels compelled to take his revenge on it. He appears a reborn CheGuivara to them. When they find any outlaws firing at police and the army they imagine Garibaldi's brown shirted men fighting in Chhattisgarh jungles in India,killing the occupying forces. Or when they find a group shouting for freedom 'Azadi' in a college or a university like the JNU; notorious for breeding effete outdated leftist and communal ideas they believe it is some oppressed,exploited people waiting for their Mazzini or a Lenin to lead them against a despotic autocracy.Finally each one of them feels compelled by emotional surges as by their funding agency to imagine their own selves to be these haloed leaders all in one combined and they pose for press photographs and make loud speeches becoming of those great revolutionaries. The problem is that their words and actions are repugnant to the silent majority and distresses them. But they watch quietly! When all great nations,from US to Britain,China to Russia are turning more and more 'nationalistic' and building walls,trade walls,social and psychological barriersand lately even concrete walls to protect their interests, all these wise men/fools want to break up their own country and nationalityand swim against the currant.They can't see that a fundamentalist invasion is already waging in their home and 7th century laws and justice system is sought to be installed wherein intellectuals of all hues themselves will be the first to be decimated.Great thinkers were not needed in Syria.Oh, I forget,it is their funding agency that determines their thinking.True helplessness!

Still further we can discern conspiracies by highly qualified people called 'Economists'. It is a known fact that ups and downs called booms and busts are an inbuilt part of capitalist economy and economists have never been able to give a cause of these and never, never and that is amusing to note, never been able to give a specific remedy.Yet they dole out advice. "Create demand", for goods over-produced by private business-men. How? By starting new Govt. factories and big projects, they reply. But you have been asking for privatization of what-ever remains of Government assets? When American president Roosevelt started his 'New economic programme' after the great depression with mega-projects like Tennessy valley project and other relief works, etc. you dubbed him a communist. Sir, what do you exactly want? Confused?

Economics,as a common man understands it,is a science of finance/money but it has been turned into a science for moneyed business men in keeping with capitalist theory. Students of economics are accordingly subjected to this brain washing and indoctrination that they exist only for big business and must see that it thrives. But unfortunately they act as rumor-mongers during downslides in economy in keeping with the worries of their rich. Patrons. In the process they snatch away the common man's peace of mind and his night's sleep, without knowing what is happening.

Their words cause disaffection in the people against the governments in power and even generalized panic. Organized economist gangs like the IMF and world bank have in the past spearheaded violent overthrow of many governments in many countries and presently they armtwist smaller nations to start 'Structural reforms' meaning sale of public assets to private business. A similar role is played world-wide by economics-churning business houses called 'the Rating Agencies' All of these are subversive to common peace. But, 'All for the good of poor and the downtrodden! We can be assured.

Closer home are many social and religious groups, NGOs etc. that can affect our lives and disturb us mentally and one ought to keep an eye! on these too.

Animals that we basically are, man has ever been an enemy of man's peace. But an informed man is no less an armed man. He remains prepared and a master of his situation!

Chapter III

<u>POETIC PLEASURES</u>

After a long pause may we go back to the subject of Adam and Eve as we had proposed and also to the relation that bound them and continues to do so ever. That relation was/is of love; **of Romantic love and I quote Bertrand Russell in praise of the same:**

"I believe myself that romantic love is the source of
the most intense delights
That love has to offer. In the relation of a man and a
woman who love each
Other with passion and imagination and tenderness,
there is something of
Inestimable value, **to be ignorant of which is a
great misfortune for any humanBeing."**

I too am a votary of the great Philosopher and it gives me unbounded pleasure to look back and imagine the taste of that sweet honey which flows from its eternal source. A charming lady is a joy forever! The delirium she is capable of inducing is a milestone from which one can count the start of a new life. That life is one of immense joy; full of roses but many thorns too, their pricks and scratches dear and sweet, unlike any.

Ishq se tabiyatney Zeist kamazapaya,

Ekdardkidawapayie, Dard la- dawapaya!

(Romance has added its taste to my dull life; My heart ache is cured but a cureless agony has replaced that. I am restless.)

Talk to anyone who is in love and he will vehemently deny that life is purposeless or aimless. He has had a true vision of life which is hard to disbelieve. It is estimated that the initial fulminating (acute) state of attraction lasts 12 to 18 months but I for one disbelieve these calculations. Love of your lady accompanies you all your life the initial phase being dominated however by a transient sexual vigour which is of course the sweetest fruit of all fruits in the world. All in all, it appears that that love itself is one's life. You can contest my view.

It is unusual (perhaps jocular as well) to allude to love of one's wife as Romantic love but personal experience makes me to call it so. I have been intensely in love with her ever since I saw her as an 18-year-old bright playful girl. I was myself so. Our friendship continues and I remain fond of her as much as I was when we were young. I don't mind living away from the entire world only if she be with me. In fact, we seek such occasions and often run to the hills for that. At least I remain very happy then, undisturbed and in peace. Perhaps it is she who grants peace in my life. Her presence around me keeps me cool and satisfied. I don't know how to explain

my relationship to her. She has shown me the most
glorious joyful moments of my life. Her name is Bimla
but I call her 'Mem'; meaning a gracious English lady.
A word of caution:
May one remember the name of Egyptian Pharaoh
Akhanaton who invented 'the one and only one god
religion', first (later copied by other Abrahmic religions
in neighborhood—in Jerusalem and Mecca). His name
has been made famous in history for a different reason as
well, by H.G. Wells, as a person who loved his beautiful
wife too much. Yet another name is already well known
for his uxoriousness (Excessive Love of one's wife) and
that is Emperor Shah Jahan. (He is disliked by his
coreligionists essentially because he loved his wife more
than he loved God, if at all)
And when you find me in company of such wife-loving
emperors I don't think you will ridicule me much for
praising and of being overmuch fond of my wife. But all
this does not mean that I never looked at any other lady
around or they did not attract or please me. A person,
who owns a very beautiful garden himself and tends to
it, can never refuse to look at other's gardens or refuse to
lend help. As a matter of fact, he loves other well-kept
gardens equally well and truly appreciates their worth. It
is beyond him to stop himself in his pursuit. It is in his
blood. He is a fond person and no one should refuse his
benevolent fondness. He is perhaps a man from a

different world who has no attraction for the pur of a note counting machine, the jingle of coins and the clang of gold bricks. Singing of a stream rushing down a green hill and the roar of a waterfall has a deep meaning for him and he understands and values these. He has an aim, a god given aim; enjoying the beauty of life in whichever form that presents; a butterfly sipping nectar from the flower, never harming it. He is more sinned against than sinning. It is seldom realized that he is assigned a role no less important; of a color on the canvas of life, a contrast colour without which other colors will look dull and drab. He is an artist who worships art; as much stunned by a beautiful piece of sculpture or a fine life like painting as by a beautiful lady. He is a devotee of everything good and he worships it. A beautiful lady, a lush green forest with tall pines waving their heads in the jungle breeze, by their hissing sound begging you to come nearer to love them, a rivulet rushing down a hill and the sound of mermaids that you can hear then; nothing but magic.

In ancient Greece they celebrated beauty in all its forms and that is how they created stunning statues and their immemorial architecture. Male body was as much praised and valued; it's beauty of form and strength and handsomeness as the delicacy and charm of an attractive female. Greek and Roman statues of males as of females compel a person to surrender his ego and to bow his head and to accept the supremacy of art over everything else. These often have a hypnotic power. Then how can anyone close his eyes or stop his ears. Please have some mercy!

It may be interesting to note that homosexuality was an accepted norm with Greek aristocracy. Parents would often encourage their sons to make themselves look presentable and handsome and then offer their services to some high noble gentleman. This they considered helpful to develop high contacts for their sons as a means to go up in life.

Doesn't the earlier description about beauty make you to realize that beauty itself is restless and impatient for appreciation otherwise how come the pines, the gushing streams and the snow clad mountains around and dazzling flowers, all are waiting and waiting indefinitely in time to be seen and enjoyed and appreciated with a 'Hoy',

'Wah, wah'. That is nature's way!

HazaroonsaalNargis (a Flower-Narcissus Poetica)

apnibenoori (Charmlessness) par Roti hai,

Badimushkil se hotahaichaman (Garden) main deedawar

(An appreciator of beauty)Paida. (AlamaIqbaal)

(Beauty awaits its lover and connoisseur infinitely and perpetually; but finds one such if at all, with difficulty)

What after all is the life of an attractive flower, born and lying alone in the wilderness of a desert. None to appreciate, none to applaud and none to enjoy and to go mad after it's scent and looks. Born to wither away unseen, unsung and unmourned! When princess Diana died the entire world was shocked, when Jacqueline Kennedy married an old Greek business tycoon, half the world was shaken and felt the loss. Beautiful women are conscious of their value and also the fact of its date of expiry, which alas is very short and so, would be happy to be appreciated and enjoy the thrill of the process when the blood is still warm but for our narrow minded society. Remove it's mental block (of your society) and everyone will feel happier! One thing, however, must be said. There is a shortage of true appreciators and connoisseurs of beauty and natural charm; those who have an eye for it. The rifraf confuses it for sex appeal and exploits it so and that is the modern method; the American way of quick solutions and that is the bane of present day society. Our feelings and ways were different from the western. Even our marriage was not a contract but an understanding, understanding of each other. In the above quoted lines from Iqbal see the importance given to the lover (Appreciator of value). It is truly difficult to love, if one understands what is meant. "areyzaraekdafakisi par mar ke to dekho" **(Just try to die for someone and then see).** Unfortunately, white colour of the skin is mistaken for beauty now. A colourful butterfly is no less beautiful than a white one, each has her own grace and attraction; just see how each flutters and flies away, taking one's heart with it.

 We had a girl from Tamil Nadu studying ayear ahead of us in the medical college. She was not white but typically of Indian make and colour; her unbraided fluttering hair reaching her hips. Her features made to perfection. Her slender neck proportionate to her height, bright hypnotizing eyes with long eyelashes fanning them and her gait, how to describe? She stepped on springs with body and head lifted softly in waves, to move forward and imagine those clouds, unbraided and floating, waving and whispering behind her, how many did she kill. How many hearts lay strewn in her path as she carelessly went her way? Careless careful beauty! That grace unseen before, nothing less than the butterflies, that we talked about above. Was she a 'Gopi' dancing for her 'Shyam sunder' Krishna; the Ghanshyam (cloud coloured Krishna) on the Yamuna banks in Vrindhawan some moments away. Yes, beauty is eternal and the cycle must continue!
English language doesn't lend itself to poetry appreciated by Asians. There are two couplets in Urdu that befit the occasion:

 "Khuda jab Hussundetahai,Nazakat aa hi jatihai" !

(Where god bestows beauty, Delicacy and grace automatically join in). She was all 'Nazakat'(delicacy) only.

This one about her hair:

"Neend us ki, dimaag us ka, raatein us kehain,Terizulfainjiskibazu par pareshan ho gayin"

(A refreshing sleep, a fresh jovial mind and colourful nights are the reward for one, whose arm you choose to rest your head [hair] upon)

A great poet has chosen Egyptian ladies as the most beautiful in the world. He is perhaps right. They have the right body contours and face lines to recommend them. Their nose is indeed poetic. But our Indian ladies are perhaps second to none and lately winning Miss World titles year after year, confirms our presumption. But the material we are talking about is such that parochialism and patriotism crumble to pieces at the mere sight of it, come she may where ever from. Beauty transcends borders and divisions; it is universal. I am, however concerned about our young men. They seem confused!

Dressing and self-grooming and beautifying has been considered natural for women. It stems from their unconscious psychological need to attract the best of men and so the best of genes for a better progeny. Hence the demand for skin whitening and colour creams. But many boys have out smarted them now in facial makeups and hair do's. Skin tight dresses to reveal their body lines and use of ear rings no less than wearing costly neck chains and even bangles often makes them look somewhere in between. Do our women fall for such stuff? In past times men showed themselves chivalrous and gallant to win a woman's heart. Has effeminacy become the latest craze? Women to ponder! Surveys reveal them seeking security and status with handsomeness, not bangled effi-males.

Above we said that the world was shocked by the death of Princess Diana or surprised and even felt a sense of disgust at Jacqueline's marriage to that Greek old man. Does anybody think about the 'Why' of these general feelings? No! Perhaps we don't have time nor any inclination to go that deep into matters which don't concern us. But it can be shown that there is some thing interesting and jovial too about such matters.. We know that nothing happens without a cause. To know about that cause let us turn to psychoanalysis:

Our mind has two parts; conscious and the unconscious. If someone in his conscious mind and sense tells you that he loved Diana intensely and was very fond of Jacqueline or any other v. highly placed beautiful lady and plans to get her somehow, you will call him a fool or a mad man. But our unconscious mind has a majestic bearing and thinking. It cares not for borders or boundaries, high or low status, nor for anything imaginable. It cares only for it's own pleasure. The fact of the matter is that our Unconscious minds had taken note of these both 'admirable' ladies and had high hopes of getting these both. All this unknown to the conscious person himself. But with their sudden loss, all high hopes were suddenly dashed to the ground and the inner mind got an earthquake of mourning at this sudden tragic news. The shock was so great that tremors were felt in the conscious mind too, which of course was at a loss to understand the reasons and the origin of waves of sadness because the epicenter of action lay beyond its knowledge, while the Unconscious said to itself "why did I not take chance while they were living and available."

But how and why were females who cared and knew about the two ladies sad and shaken by the events that overtook them? The explanation is slightly lengthy but interesting. So let us start by repeating that our Unconscious mind does not think in ideas or words.,but in raw emotions/affects only.Mostly it runs on two emotions only i,e love and hate-two sides of the same coin.And then we know jealousy is rampant in matters of heart.We also know that women as a class take great note of other women's dress and looks. Now imagine a scene where a stranger lady good looking and young, with a smiling face in a bright looking magenta colour Sari joins a group of ladies at a temple or church gathering.Several heads turn,many,eyes open wide,and no less noses turn up creased. Whence cometh this off - season lark?At once the question poses itself.Who will notice me while she is around?So the exemplary wife has her agenda set for the night's meeting with her husband. 'Darling since when have I been asking for that Sari? Today I have decided to get it as a gift from you on your coming birthday just 9 days to go--the same 'magenta colour sari with that hand embroidered border'.There will be many guests here that day and I will wear it. 'I have been asking for it so long' she confirms her order. This is automatic harmless jealousy. But jealousy(a hate emotion) gives place to a feeling of remorse(a love emotion) on sudden news of death of the hated object.The person's Unconscious repents for having grown unfairly sensitive towards an innocent,harmless person.So a part cause of women's sadness over Diana's death was their subtle guilt and the other part of sadness was contributed by 'identification ' with her i,e"why was I not Diana?My beauty and charm would at long last have been seen and recognized by all the world.Haaye,what a death? In the arms of her lover,dressed in royal costume,swishing in a special class merc!Who wouldn't have liked to be in her place?

And today they would be repenting over my death,not having valued me when I was living.I wish it was me; I am really sad for her ".If confronted she would say,Lo! where was she-a princess and where my poor self?Am I mad to compare myself with her?How could I be jealous of her,she was too good and gentle,yes,yes she was very gentle...though I am also quite gentle.And beautiful too.Of course her regal dress and make-up gave her that shape to a great measure.And then the press extoled her looks and figure.I am younger in years than her,that also counts after all!It is said,'whom gods love die soon'.And I am really sorry, I agree she was surely fit for the Gods only,she was so good,I fully agree.(a sting in the tail—she was not fit for men?)

It is even now not difficult to discern a tinge of jealousy towards the Greek old man when Jaqulin's name comes up for discussion for some reason, mostly connected with her marriage which gave happiness to no one who knew her. The name of the Greek 'Onassis' is also remembered or recognized by many because of the connection it got with their 'beautiful ladylove of our unconscious mind' which has still not forgotten the shock which he gave it. A well-read patient of mine once called him 'omnesis'- the man who married "that lady with her beautiful white hat". Asked to correct the name he said 'Onemesis'. Finally, he accepted with a loud laughter the correction 'Oh, Nemesis' (Death) for the Greek tycoon. He did not know that he actually wished him death. Such is the working of our subconscious mind and such is how analysis proceeds. It needs much study and knowledge, time, patience, practice and perseverance.

 Back to beauty of life: And reminded of '**Nargis**' by Iqbal's couplet, I must talk of our famed actress Nargis also. She too was an unknown beautiful flower but its blossom was invoked as if by magic when she met the great artist and connoisseur of beauty in Raj Kapoor. I was a fan of both. Look at the emblem of RK. Films-Raj holding an ecstatic arched Nargis on his one arm, watching her while holding a guitar in his otherhand; the guitar, music, yet another sacred source and compass and a symbol of the heights of self-refinement the humans can achieve. What a confluence! What heights of art and depths of thought? All life melts in to this one symbol of our raw existence. Just give it a thought! 'A loaf of bread and a jug of wine and thou beside me' by the great poet Omar Khayam, pales in comparison to describe the state of bliss achieved thus. 'Empowerment of women' by giving them jobs and money and in particular seats in legislatures, is the current slogan in the air. One would instead call for 'Independence to women'-their long suppressed souls, by ensuring every woman'seducation. Give the female soul itsfreedom, empowerment will automatically follow. The famous song depicting the 'red Russian cap on head and the poor Japani boot below, in one stroke depicts human history and the thought that dominated the first three quarters of twentieth century. It is not a mere song to be muttered in a bathroom; it had a deep symbolic significance for the times we sailed in. Just give this too a moment's thought! Then was a time of love. Time when man loved man, when poor, the deprived and the hungry were thought about, Socialism was in the air and everything smelled of love. Emblem of RK films was born in that period and depicts nothing but love. (Awarahoon). Raj Kapoor was one of the greatest art masters of the century and he worshiped at the altar of Aphrodite (the goddess of love). His productions elaborated and explained the sentiment of the times, the aspirations of a poor people and the real place of woman in life. He was a great intellectual. Indians when told of Raj kapoor usually retort 'He caricatured some Charlie Chameleon' not knowing that their Charlie was ultimately disgraced and compelled to run away from U.S. Dark skin inferiority! Please don't berate your own great men and also never underestimate a woman. Liberate her soul through good education. She is provided as a means for human upliftment through joy and pleasure often sacrificing her own self.

Man and woman, Adam and Eve, Hermes and Aphrodite, each compliments the other and also brings out the best in each; that is the natural way. Would Nargis have flowered the way she did if Raj would not have met her. Main ingredient in the process was apparently the amorous love they developed for each other. It honed up both; they put in their best for the sake of each other and out of that the humanity benefitted; grew richer. Go and ask any Russian of that period still living and he still remembers 'Rita' and 'Raj' of Awara film. She became a joy and heart throb of millions. Thanks to the innate relation of Adam and Eve. She was already a cut and polished diamond when Mehboob took her up for his 'Mother India'.

Mad with love: While I speak of beauty an impression is perhaps created that I am praising female beauty overly. That is perhaps natural because I happen to be a man. It is in my blood and God given. But please give the following couplet (an excerpt from a popular film song of 1950's), a thought:

"Mastibharijawani,yehhussunyehshabab, (Uuph, My bubbling youth and this glow of beauty;these pulsating desires,)
Rangeendilkimehfil, mere haseinkhwab"! (Andwhat of the colourful world of my heart and my magnificent dreams!)

There is a slant of femininity in these words but they were popular with all. Because they found an echo in every heart, male as well female-a universal cry of life. Even now, when quoted, they resonate in every heart. A hundred lives for that brief but joyful glimpse of one's inner self!

Now tell me if there is anything indecent, obscene or immoral about this basic human appeal for joy and self-actuation. These words incite a torrent of joy; a life time of joy felt in one single moment in the very depths of heart.

It is difficult to get the emotion behind this couplet into a translation because it describes something more than female or male beauty. It describes the eternal feminine and the eternal masculine urges, if you conceive it so. Beauty appreciated that way is as indescribable as perhaps is the infinite life itself because it then is a part of that same infinite. It is however represented or symbolized for the male by a female and vice versa and we find it natural to project these urges onto these representations. And these representations are most of the times idealistic and utopian! But very important in the conduct of our life. So, egged on by the same eternal urges if I remain biased towards the feminine, is that a fault; any sin? These also happen to be the unending source of man's poetic and artistic imagination. O, this world has grown dull and insipid. Look at the creation around you. How the butterfly is never tired of fanning cool air on the petals of a rose-it's cheeks, blushing and burning pink and red with the hot 'stuff of life', like a maiden who blushes at every little event and cause and even on no cause, knowing not how to conceal her 'stuff of life', her innermost desires. Different flowers colour themselves differently only to hide their hot blushed cheeks and the deep secrets (Of murder?) they keep; I tell you on the authority of a poet who knows them intimately. So please give this a thought and believe it truly. They all, including the shy damsel stand for and are awaiting that moment of their self-actuation and self-realization, that moment of greatest appreciation that calms one's restless soul. The beatle at the merest flicker of light in a dark night grows mad, and restless hovers, hums and buzzes singing it's love in the ears of the flame begging oneness and merger, the final bliss and ultimate ecstacy. Look deeper and one finds the whole universe is in love and stands governed by love. What are called forces of magnetism, of electric charges and gravity etc. by the careless uninitiated throng are but the cruder perceptions and different names for the same force and power of love, so said the same poet. Have I grown mad? Not entirely perhaps, for I can still hear the sensible, soothing and sweet words of John Keats traversing two hundred years of time:

"Beauty is truth, truth beauty;
That is all ye know on earth and all ye need to know".
I have neither it nor words nor even the power to compose them to say a 'Hurrah' to the renowned poet.
But my heart dares to whisper:
'Beauty unloved, unsung goes waste,
Truth untold, no less;
Love to both gives life and taste.
So I love ye and all, post-haste!
(DhayeeAkhisherpremke….). Just four syllables…,
'LOVE' COMPRISES WHOLE OF LEARNING.

The truth of the whole saga of man's life probably is that **this is essentially a woman's world**, created around woman, for woman and at the instance, overt or covert, of woman. Men are under a universal delusion that they are building for themselves. They are mere mercenaries compensated differently at different times. And they are happy! Wha-at? --fools? Not wholly, they are wise fools! They sip nectar from flowers and are content. Worker bees!

Pascal, a great philosopher, scientist and writer, among others perhaps realized this fact when he wrote that world history would have been different had Cleopatra's nose been different.

Historically, men would have been living a nomadic life but for the woman. She makes a home, many homes combine to form a hamlet, many hamlets combine to form a village and then a city and then the whole world and the hunter nomadic man takes to agriculture to industry, makes laws to safeguard all that she initiated and we call ourselves civilized. I remember having slept one night on newspaper sheets spread on bare Howrah railway station platform, as a bachelor. Can I do that now with my woman along? NO. I have now built a house for 'MYSELF' and I show that to all my acquaintances as 'my house'. All fooling! The truth in practice stands that it is she who somehow without uttering a word, compelled me to build that house FOR HER and FOR her brood. I never needed one and would certainly not have toiled for it. I was a carefree person and any other railway or bus platform could have served my purposes the best. It is most wonderful of nature that even this our 'all-powerful woman' is in dark about what is happening at her behest and for her sake. Without any hue and cry She has made all that difference in my life while I never even suspected the real design and her involvement in it. Her world!

Any well earning bachelor can buy or construct a house for himself. Thereafter instead of his lodge or hotel as was earlier the case, he now lives a more independent carefree life, coming back from office in evenings to his house with a pride and a sense of achievement and mastery. Just because he owns the place. Now enter Woman! Lo, the house becomes his 'home', overnight. Now he comes back in evenings to his 'home' and even has a feeling of hurry in doing so. Come rain, snow or any blizzard, he braves that to reach his home even earlier, lest she being alone and so inconvenienced in anyway. Earlier he would stay the night at some friend's place falling on the way. Now he wants to reach home somehow. It is an entirely different feeling. A definiteness of a 'destination 'the earlier one reaches the more satisfying! And this is NOTEWORTHY. The man has found his destination-through the woman. If he be imaginative he soon knows that even he, his very self has changed; his role in the 'House' has suddenly changed. Soon finds out that the place feels different, much has already changed therein. Even the cold inanimate walls are recognised and are felt emanating a sense of ownness and warmth; they have started talking and you unconsciously react, equally with a feeling of nearness and love. The house has been magically changed!

See, how woman infuses into the cold walls of a house, pulsating life, vitality and warmth. And though she herself also feels and perceives the insidious change occurring around, she paradoxically doesn't know and understand that it is she who is the agent for it. Vulgar feminists ought to note this central position of women in homes and how women are 'The' real masters' and owners of their homes and not the exploited drudges they make people to believe they are. New brides feel their psychological change the most and unexpectedly when they return to parental house even after just a few days of their marriage. They find the house and everything around gone strange; that old love for things dearly owned thus far has lost intensity; a distance having crept in. Magic show of womanhood has changed stage and venue!

Now my dear young men, what else do you want from these angles? To be slim, delicate charming and attractive for you plus maintain your home, entertain your guests, look after your aged parents, cook, bear your children, bring them up and then supervise their education, teach them the way to their life, entertain you after you come home from office and at night to warm your bed. AND NOW, and. now, also to go out to labour during the day in some office or some work site in order to earn and pay her share in the new found partnership. And per chance if she earns more than your earning, you grow jealous of her. And there from often starts the discord that mars manysuch partnerships- 'for-profit' among uncounted earning couples. And most often it is the males that start the fire.

Marriages in India used to have a different and perhaps one lone aim and purpose: to bring up a pleasant home through division of labour crowned by cooperative effort; the male for the male job and the delicate angel looking after and utilizing for the commune what was brought home by the husband from his labour. Do ladies look like having been built for hard labour and round the clock service? Please ponder! And if any lady chooses to do so for betterment of her home, then she must be encouraged and recognition of her service must follow in the form of love and special respect for her.

I dare say out of my life's experience that behind every happy home there must always be a satisfied woman It cannot be otherwise. A woman is happy if she, like all others, feels loved and needed and so cared for. But then her story is different from others. Nature has given her an innate capacity to transmit her own happiness, multiplied many fold to other family members, in many fold ways, seen as well as unseen by the husband.

Yet another factor that compels women to labour outside their homes, especially during the early days when they are establishing their new home, is the eye the couple jointly keep on their neighbours and the tormenting wish to outdo them and the other relatives in material achievements. The temptations of the consumerist society and the induced need for all things advertised for the 'ideal home and an ideal life', are no less responsible for grinding work regimens forced by women upon their selves. O, one only wishes that people could realistically assess their life requirements and act in accordance. As stated else-where it does not take too much money to live peacefully and in real comfort.

During my early employment days our pay was by present standards ridiculously low and now a laughable sum. But I remember, none of us;dozens of us, never felt the pinch of poverty or ever looked around at rich men to grow jealous of them. Stranger, we never talked of an ambition of growing rich. Yes, we often talked about post-graduation and how to go around for that. No inviting advertisements induced us to think of acquiring more. (In fact there was no TV then and so no visual mouth-watering attractions of cheese-burst pizzas and the like). Birla's and Tatas were the common examples, given of really rich people during common conversation, and it would naturally be futile growing jealous of them; they were practically beyond reach. Life was peaceful and simple. Also an inbuilt paradox of that 'green' jealousy; one can only be jealous of people near you, not of Bill gates. He is praised for his intelligent ways and how he is so rich, but your brother or neighbour if he is just slightly better off is a constant irritant of your mind.In our acquaintance there were not many people much better than us, or if there were any they never flaunted their wealth. 'Showing off' is a new method in times. Earlier it was considered immodest! People also thought of the poor. Air was unpolluted, clean. No Capitalist greed no exploitation, no display!

Enter Laxmi (Hindu Godess of wealth). Same house surgeons (Young doctors) are paid thousands-in wads. They have many around who earn in lacs, even more-far far more. Many inherit great riches. etc. So heart burning is the new disease. Every one of the middle class has something solid, at least available in easy instalments to build upon, only how and what to build viz 'the technology and the blue print' are lacking. So any richer relative, a neighbour, living in a posh bungalow are easy examples to emulate and to outdo. Consumerist advertisements and forced selling of luxury goods come handy to help. Technology of richness sells free; indeed, a great achievement of age. And so the rat race. Both male as well as the female are welcome. Buy one, get one free!

More about the females: Thank God, the human female is the only one perhaps who doesn't have an oestrus the 'heat' in her sexual life or else she would run away in search of mating partners like so many animals and the superstructure that man has built for her would not have come about. Female sexual behavior   is subtle and soft in comparison to male which is aggressive, demanding and even rough. While males take a delight in showing their private parts to their women the latter are not very pleased by the action except during first meetings wherein curiosity plays a part. One exhibitionist (people who show their private parts to opposite sex for pleasure) can send away shrieking and crying a full hall of women all in shock. After marriage it is a common taunt for husbands by the wives that they are only after sex, while there are many other ways in which a woman derives equal satisfaction, far away from actual coitus, primarily what assures her that her man cares for her and loves her. In fact, a woman feeling assured in her heart about her man's love often submits to his demands as a reward for his good behavior and not for her own self primarily. Her own reward and pleasure appear secondary to her in this process of love. It may appear curious to know that a female even during the actual act of love- making, consciously or unconsciously keeps watching facial and other cues from the man to determine whether he has enjoyed the act or not. A satisfied man helps her ego and she feels a more complete woman within, in her ability to give good pleasure and satisfaction to her man. Many women seldom feel an orgasmic delight in mating still they engage in it simply to give pleasure to their man. A woman is temperamentally the most malleable and soft possession of man and the Shakespearean Quote 'Frailty thy name is woman' if understood in the right sense is a compliment to womanhood. It praises their bio-psychological make. Strong self-willed women don't make peaceful homes.

Regarding sexual orgasm, it is interesting to note that the intensity of orgasmic pleasure in coitus appears to be proportional to one's ability to surrender to one's partner at that time and that perhaps depends on one's fondness and liking for him or her, as the case may be. This applies more to females than to males, it is observed. At the height of pleasure some people perhaps feel like dying and some even cry out 'oh, I am dead'. This is a psychological equivalent of what our long forgotten ancestors did in reality long ago in the process of evolution. They would actually die out after mating. At the physiological (Bodily) level this is represented by a brief spell of unconsciousness and lack of memory for the event. At one's conscious psychological level the process takes the shape of an unconditional and total surrender which is perceived sweet and delicious. More so in case of females. Accordingly, a prominent component **of female inorgasmia** could be an inability to surrender to the partner.

In Italian, there is a saying that a **woman is like a guitar** and it is for her man to derive and play which tune he wants to and can. In sex life, woman is subject to peculiar ways and behavior depending upon how her man wants it and so teaches her. Accordingly, no two sexual acts between two couples are ever the same. Many perverse methods and means are employed for the same act of pleasure and it is surprising that even highly qualified women, often doctors and biologists are unaware about how unnatural their method of play is. Worse, that they don't even feel the unnaturalness and perversity of their actions. They consider it normal and while talking about it to their doctor feel no hesitation, because they have been trained to accept that as a normal thing. I will give a **small example:**

 A young man, after about 18 months of his marriage reports that he suffers from premature ejaculation and that his bride reports not feeling any sensation of semen falling within her. He further confirmed that all his discharge falls on the bed clothes. Is your wife satisfied by your performance? He replies, "She is happy". Is your erection good? "Yes". One day he comes saying that they consulted a gynecologist about her failure to feel his discharge and the doctor revealed to them that the wife's hymen was unbroken. Consequently, I asked that he bring her along to me which he hesitatingly did after some further dilly dally. She was a sprightly charming and smiling lady working as a lecturer in biology and during the interview it was known that the boy would simply lodge his organ between her thighs and had never attempted a penetration. But the girl was quite satisfied and happy and only worried about the wastage of semen and so was ready to blame her own receptacle and biology of parts.

Now see a biology lecturer is happy with such a sexual performance because her man tells her that he is fully satisfied and admired her for that. Her life's aim of being a fit woman is fulfilled, the man having certified that. Her only worry was about semen wastage, perhaps because she thought it would in the long run result in her childlessness. (Bearing a child, preferably a male one is another and final certificate of her worthiness as a woman). The couples had to be guided on the right course and are happier now.

In the first sentence of the above Para I have used the word 'Admired' and this takes me to an interesting **explanation for admiration.** This is psychoanalytic of course. Why do we admire someone or some quality in him or her or in something? Because we like it, so we admire that. In other words, we would like to possess or own the admired object or quality ourselves. So please remember this definition of admiration when you admire some one's bungalow, car or his pretty wife. But that is no crime if we remember as stated separately that a good gardener likes to watch and praise all beautiful gardens he sees and feels delighted by them. Won't he be all the morehappy and thankful if given a chance to help enrich the garden?

And now I think it won't be much if we try to explain human sentiment of **jealousy also.** Both admirations as well as jealousy have a common parent viz: our wish to possess the thing we admire or feel jealous of, in others. For the present, we take the case of a beautiful actress. We praise everything about her and are her devoted fans. One day however, we suddenly find that she is closeted in a room in our neighborhood with some young man and people have come to know about that and have collected in throngs around. Whosoever joins them asks them the reason for standing there and watching the building and he is informed that a young lady, some actress is having illicit relations with some man there. Lo! a cry arises, 'Call the police'. Some one more religious cries for murdering the man for violating the sacredness of womanhood and everybody joins in that pious duty. After all what example are they making in our neighborhood for our young daughters and sisters? No, no, they must both be skinned off. But someone says from behind, it cannot be the lady's fault, we know her. She is a great actress and we love her. She can't do it.

Hang the man who has compelled her for this impious act and all agree, nodding in satisfaction.

Now the psychoanalytic explanation: Jealousy of the young man and nothing else. Every one of the crowd unconsciously feels and says to himself, "I am so virile and energetic, how come this worthless sinner then? I alone deserve this beautiful actress". Every one of the pious crowd would love to possess the actress, who would not? Please note the italicized words above because these convey a very deep male sense of insecurity regarding one's own stock of valued females (This male insecurity has been of fundamental importance in creating our civilization.). He wants to safeguard them first, as his eyes scan around for his own interests and purpose. This, of course, is an analytic view.

As we are on the subject nearly, I must talk about 'Feminism' too. **Feminist cry or movement** essentially is about seeking equal opportunities and rights for women visa vis men. No doubt laudable and in keeping with the times! And every sensible person will vote for it. But some strange things are observable on the scene. Some very highly placed women in life notably MDs and CEOs of big corporations are not free from this feminist grievance against male domination in society. Yet none of them are known to have addressed this complaint in their empires despite their power to do so. What have our all-powerful PMs likeIndiraji and Thatcher etc. done about the problem? Don't criticize me if it is said that perhaps feminists and females in general, themselves don't know what they actually are clamoring for. Psychoanalysis perhaps has an answer.

This is at heart a jealousy of males who have for all practical purposes monopolized the freedom to sow wild oats as and where they please. In psychoanalysis it is called P…. envy. I know of no feminist except **Inessa Armand** who had a special place in Lenin's heart and so could afford to be courageous and so succinctly and openly verbalized the grievance in a letter to her paramour asking for right of "freedom to love" to be accepted by the proletarian state. She was a known feminist and hit the bull's eye. But the all-time egalitarian Valadimir Lenin, that great equalizer of humans turned down her request declaring it a "Bourgeois demand". Despicable Male chauvinism!

Innessa did not give up. She, herself a married woman, wrote him a clarification saying that she had not demanded 'freedom for adultery'. Lenin apparently was silent.

And she also had to keep quiet. Traditional female modesty and patience-born out of unconscious impulses!

But one thing at least is clear; Inessa unlike other shy, reticent and often ignorant modern feminists didn't beat round the bush. She knew the actual and most essential female grievance. It appears that women in general are more reticent about their real wishes for fear of being branded immoral and ill charactered by the jealous males. Innessa had a tolerant lover with whom she naturally had no such fears.

It should not be difficult to discern what lay behind her 'not asking for freedom of adultery'. In fact that was her actual motivation both conscious as well as unconscious. It may not be wrong to state that this is a general if not a universal finding. Adultery like the forbidden apple is considered by many to be far more interesting and a pleasurable adventure. Every bit of the story around it is in- itself an absorbing tale; a tale of two yearning and beating hearts all the time apprehensive of what may happen next. A sword keeps hanging over the head of actor's every time. Suspense provided by stealth in word as well in deed makes it exhilarating. It involves much daredevilry often and so the tale fulfils all requirements of an interesting drama both for its actors and the listeners if any.

In olden times, husbands of supposed adulterous women, called cuckolds were believed to grow horns on their head; in short it was considered a slur. Things may be as they are, freedom of adultery can rock the very foundations of the society and the civilization that humans have developed with much sacrifice and emotional control. Lenin perhaps did realize this and so kept quiet.

It is perhaps not unsafe; and instead could be interesting to speculate that had the demand for freedom of love been somehow accepted and the natural P-factor in females annulled somehow in right early time, women of power also would have maintained their male harems. And Nizam of Hyderabad would perhaps not have been the last and the only important person around to do so. Also matrilineal family structure (with mother as chief controller) of past ages would not have easily given place to the prevailing patriarchal society (Father as family boss). And bridegrooms instead of the brides would go to live at their in-laws and stay subservient to the fabled mother-in-law, property also being at stake.

Other thing apart, Inessa like most 20th century revolutionaries was an intellectual. Russian socialist revolutionaries then were a highly read and knowledgeable lot, not laloo's, aloo's and Rahul's, shahul's and mayajals who thrive on cheating people in the name of caste and religion. Most lived for a greater cause and have left much readable literature beside their excellent examples of a meaningful life.

As is my habit I shall deviate again from my path a little to say something about two great men: It appears that George Bernard Shaw had wished that a man's life time ought to have been three hundred years at least. When Sigmund Freud heard this, he vehemently opposed the idea saying that it would be bad for humans in the long run and our age as fixed by nature is perfect. Great men won't give advice or opinion unsolicited and it looks as if God had asked for opinion on the subject from these two of the greatest of men and so they were debating on it in earnest. But God seems to have withheld his final judgment on the issue so far. And this gives a commoner (a proletarian) like me a chance to submit his opinion too, though unsolicited. And so I submit that all men aged 78 now should be afforded one more chance to restart their lives at age 28. They should be given a remission of 50 years. In support of my appeal I quote Mirza Ghalib's famous couplet:

Hazaroonkhahisheinaiseikiharkhahish par dhamnikle
Bade nikle mere armanlekinfirbhikamnikle.

(Thousands of **Killer desires** fill my heart, many, many are fulfilled but thousands more lie craving within me.)

A few words about 'Killer desires': Instant death is the reward for their actual realization; no spark left, Oh boy it doesn't start, no life, dead? But they are the most murderous; they throttle you if left unfulfilled. Murder either way. Actual victims will please attest!

And if given a chance to be young again I solemnly promise that I will stride mountains, ride the rough seas and fly like a bird to all corners of this beautiful and wonderful earth, and above all will show these present day young men the true worth of their youth. Living through TV screens and smart phones is hardly real life. It is a delusion! Further I promise to die a fully satisfied man if given a chance to live amidst pine trees in a jungle where I will watch my lovely wild animals, roaming around freely, every morning and evening. My imagination is running amuck perhaps, but must quickly admit that I feel mildly jealous; just a little jealous of young people as I see them around, active and kicking, making merry; something that has been snatched from me while I was not watchful. My youth simply slipped away while I was careless asleep. Foolishness is a major component of youth, I realize. And overconfidence is the feathered cap that foolishness often wears!

Nevertheless, I must feel satisfied that I have played my innings and many, really many, pleasant hits, catches and runs I do recollect and remember with delight. I now laugh at the falls, bruises, cuts even the bones broken in the game. All healed. And I am 78, not out. Ready!

Nature has been very kind to me in many ways or may be because I am habitually a dreaming kind I find it interesting and joyful to live on the 'border'. It has been a 'mixed'-nature cum nurture but delightful experience. All up to you how you take it; that is the essence.

The word 'nature' connotes a static, passive and an inactive state of existence around; on the other hand, what one finds in reality is a dynamic, active and a feeling and sensible, vibrant pulsating and breathing reality that surrounds us. Perhaps thesanskrit word 'Prakrati' describes the state more aptly. She seeks you! She is actually living and calls out to you to appreciate her, taste her. I often am reminded of the famous film producer V. Shantaram's picture 'Navrang' wherein the main character finds the heroine, aptly called 'Mohini'- the female principle of eternal attraction; Goddess Aphrodite dancing and singing in myriad shapes, forms and colors, everywhere and all around, in air, on the ground, in the gushing streams of crystal clear water, on treetops and in the green foliage around. That is what one's beloved also does for those who know her value. She sings and dances to please you, to myriad tunes, at unthought-of frequencies and channels and the beauty lies in the fact that one can find her whenever one needs her. You will say, this fool has been shadow-boxing!

Any way I must talk a little more of 'Mohini' and say that a woman is essentially a vessel carrying within itself the attributes of the eternal feminine and all the potentiality of revealing the entire cosmic beauty and the meaning of life unto a man. I am not a traditional religious man but do appreciate the concept of 'Natraja'- the dancing god Siva, amongst Indians. It is fascinating. I don't know whether Hellens(early Greeks) who were no less imaginative, also had thought of any dancing Gods for themselves. It underscores the dynamic changing and transforming beauty of cosmos, infact its very nature.A dancing God balancing himself constantly during his movements perhaps symbolizes the self-adjusting vast ecosystem that, this universe happens to be.

The hero in the above said film is a man of poetic temperament who gets married to a common village belle,rustic but extraordinarily pretty.This is what triggers the emotional tsunamiin him and he goes around singing lyrics in her praise, imagining her dancing to his tunes and utterances where ever he looks.The shapes and the myriad colors of the beauty of life are revealed to him by andthrough her!

Where words fail to convey,where they can't reach, music does and dance does it more effectively.These are more primordial and more native forms of feeling and communication,developed and perfected far earlier than the use of language, during our evolution.The power of para-lingual communication and it's development in many persons can be judged for example, by Napoleon's declaration that he never used arms to destroy his enemies and opponents but demolished them with his eyes.Similarly,many people report feeling peaceful and happy sitting in presence of good and saintly men.An encounter with a jolly,happy-go-lucky fellow often makes others too happy.It infects.The world of emotion is extremely vast and deep.Often times ,in our day-to-day lives too we find that our tongue does not convey our message fully and well and then we use our hands,facial gestures,eye movements,head and even our foot and leg movements to convey what we actually mean.Going a step further all these body movements and gestures have been put to use collectively and properly patterned and that is called 'Dance'.Hip gyrating and thrusting are crude attempts at exhibiting crude passions and have not been encouraged in Indian dancing.The dancing Siva, the 'Nataraja'expresses the ultimate and otherwise difficult to express infinitesimal reality— 'Truth and Beauty'as sung by John Keats. Its message is not for eyes and ears only but for one's heart and even his soul direct.And for this to happen the receiving antennae have to stay properly adjusted.In such a cultivated state,for example, the ordinary man-woman relationship is not a mere stop-gap,boredom-relieving exercise but becomes a celebration,a conscious continuous celebration of the charms of life.We have tried to hint at this conscious celebration of love and beauty earlier too.After all a meeting between an intellectually and emotionally well-developed man and his woman has necessarily to be qualitatively and in concept and substance different from the meeting between a bull and his cow,A man you will remember,for example, continues to remember the innocent looks and the magical shy but meaningful smile of a flower like girl even after 60 years of its appearance for a mere 2 to 3 minutes in his life.He has in the process harvested bushels full of joy from it.More so he joyously describes such events of his life before his friends and the near-by both young and old,making them laugh at life's patterns and it'skaleidoscopic colors.In return such incidents often evoke long forgotten but pleasant and at times highly emotional stories in his listeners too. Life's joy can be and should be shared!

On the other a woman at 54 years when reminded by her husband, of her youthful looks, her soft civilized coy manner of yielding to his male demands, with a smile of readiness,now feels offended. From his grim faced lady he gets this:'Has age taught us nothing?When it is time to remember God, should I remember that madness of girlhood?Should we refuse to grow up?' You know I was never interested in that dirty foolishness.I only submitted to it because of your compulsion.If the children come to know your lecherous mindset,they will ostracize you." "Hah haha, they are the children of my desires and your pious hopes;of my warm surging blood and your serene hopes.They are the cream and crest of our life.They understand me as much as I understand you.They are liberal like me and tolerate like you.",pleads the poor fellow,adding "Now look you appear as sweet and attractive to me now as you were at marriage time,." "Lo!Please get your eyes and mind tested,I was married to you 34 years ago.Good Lord, all is wasted." Now, judge for yourself please!

Concept of a silent,unconcerned God is very different from a prying god who maintains bulky ledgers of account for every individual person,making entries of their good and bad actions therein.As said earlier,this universe is a huge conscious ecosystem balancing and rebalancing itself automatically.It needs no external vigilance or help either from any God or even from a devil for it or forit's small wheels or cogs i.e., us individually to run our course.The guiding principle for this universe appears to be'Reap as you sow'.God taken merely as a conceptual figure (if there has to be one) with no reality about it has to be unconcerned and so dancing in it's own 'Dhun' or 'the music of Being'the being of millions of galaxies hurtling in space creating music that cosmic 'hum'.In such a scenario where do we count?Mere specs of matter,minute insects? And yet man imagines himself to be at the center of universe, (Ashraf-ul-Makhlookat—the best and most privileged of all creation or whatever this senseless word may convey) and God having created all the rest for his purpose and use. Some people believe that only man possesses a soul;the sheep,chicken, cow etc. etc. having none, can be slaughtered to be eaten for pleasure and taste.A tiny ant creeping on the surface of a large foot-ball would be no less imaginative.

Friends, this life is yours to live; one may do it laughing or weeping, choice is free. Remember Tennyson, Wordsworth, and Shelley among others who spoke and wrote about nature. Their words are infused by their intense passion of heart and that is why they are compelling. It is ultimately a matter of heart only; they felt it in there!
And now to blessings of romantic love.

In the mid sixteenth century, a moon; an unusually beautiful full moon was sighted/born in Kashmir valley not very far from Srinagar. She was high up, far higher than imagination can take one; she had such great attributes. A little literate but she had a poetic genius and a melodious voice in addition to her beauty which is said to have been unmatchable. Her parents, as was fated gave her the name of 'Zoon' the Kashmiri word for moon. And rightly so; she played out no less. The then king of Kashmir, Yousuf Shah Chak also saw her and was stunned by her dazzling beauty. He offered to marry her and so were married. Soon Emperor Akbar in pursuance of his aim of annexing Kashmir called Yusuf to Delhi and imprisoned him perhaps in Bihar. Zoon left alone, wept bitterly and profusely so that her torrential tears filled up all the low lying areas of Kashmir and that is how the lakes of Kashmir were formed while her overflowing tears still run in various streams and rivulets all over singing her melodious sad tunes and songs which can be heard even now. But 'conditions apply': The hearer must him/herself be in despair of love. Desolation of her lovelorn heart burst into songs depicting her pain at separation from her love and her heart rending despair .She had been renamed "HabbaKhatoon" at her marriage with the king and so the name of HabbaKhatoon is famous for the literary contribution that an illiterate genius has made to the local literature and no less for the sweet songs of love she sung then recalling her lover, that reverberate and resonate in the valley from one corner to the other and from one mountain to the other on all sides still. One of her melodies asks the lover why he has deserted her at a time when her garden of youth and beauty is in full bloom. She reminds him that it is he who owns it and only he must enjoy it. So please come soon, she begs! Bounty and bonus of love! 'Our sweetest songs are those that tell our saddest thoughts.' (Shelley).

Our scientists say that some nerve enzymes like nor epinephrine and dopamine cause the excitement and bliss that people experience in love. But excitement and a short lived bliss as it is called may not be the entirety of love. These scientific theories mostly confuse love with sex in attempts to measure and calculate and of course the eastern conceptions of these happen to be different often times. Science for example may fumble if asked to talk about beauty and its charms. If two individuals are in love should we say that the above named two enzymes of the man are reacting with their opposite enzymes vasopressin and oxytocin of the lady and that is their relationship? A queer description! A murderer can accordingly plead that it was the sudden rush of Adrenaline hormone within his body which is responsible for the deed and not he. How is he culpable? Our scientists will bear him out perhaps.

This crudity makes me reminisce **an event depicting the regality, innocent naiveté and childlike grace of pure love:** It is a long time ago we were a group of two doctors and a couple of assistants carrying out sterilization operations in various parts of Bombay. One of the Assistants happened to be a charming and really gracious American girl who was here as a Peace Corps volunteer (programme run by President Kennedy then). She was very friendly and a helpful kind and very fond of music. She even liked Indian music especially our classical one and would get lost in it despite her young age. Everyone loved her for her cheerfulness and sobriety of manner. She prepared fantastic cakes and would feed us in time of leisure. I could see she felt much happy feeding her home made delicacies to us and at times to me in particular. Sometime the person who assisted me in surgery went on leave and she immediately volunteered to assist me. But she had long nails in her hands and I objected to that on scientific grounds. The next day she comes into our makeshift operation theatre to show me her clipped nails and so I accepted her to assist me. One another day she gave me a slip of paper and I found the words 'please change your barber, he disfigures your head, please forgive me' written on it. I had got my hair cut then. Thereafter she profusely apologized to me for her unsolicited advice about my hair and we forgot the matter. Again one time while assisting me when somehow I thanked her for some good thing she did she retorted 'I didn't cut my long preserved nails for nothing; it was for you, otherwise I loved them much'. I innocently thanked her for that and so on and so forth it went on for quite some time. I also forgot to tell her name here and so must say that we did not know her real name, only everybody called her 'Mem sahib' but she would resent being called so. Accordingly, because of her maddening interest in music I had given her the name of 'Carol' meaning a song sung in churches in praise of god (Christmas carols). She had gladly accepted her renaming and the entire group called her by the same name. She called me 'Doctor'. She knew that I was a married man. All the same I found her taking much pleasure in doing whatever I wanted and would ask for the work shifts where I was there. Finally, when her term of work finished in India we gave her a small farewell party and amidst that I asked her what if any special thing she was carrying back to America, and she replied, "What I wanted I could not, except some memories I am going back empty handed". Upon insistence she revealed that she "wanted to put me in her pocket" to carry along. The subject turned at once serious and both of us blushed in full view of others and everyone got silent while a pang of sorrow descended on my heart. She was in tears. I realized I had been insensitive perhaps brutally so, not having realized the gravity of what was going on for so long and thus having encouraged her though indirectly. I said, "Oh, really sorry". The words poured really out of the depths of my heart, I don't know why! 'Ishq who aaghaijolagayenalageaurbujaynabujay' (This flame of

love; can neither be lit by force, nor if started, be put out
by effort.) It singes you any way!

Chapter IV

<u>JOY OF LIFE, A CULTIVATION OF MIND</u>

It may appear rather unbelievable to say that most of us are most of the times not as fully aware of their own selves and the world around as we ought to be. We, especially the city dwellers, have grown insensitive even towards such major natural phenomena as the changing seasons. One season is marked 'bad' and the other season 'good' just on the basis of a few degrees' temperature difference. We know of no other contrasts between various seasons. This is so in part because Indian cities lack flowering plants and shrubs in their green cover, where ever that exists. Coming and going of flowers and greenery on plants in the neighborhood is a pretty reminder to our mind about change of seasons. Also there are no trees that would change color and shed leaves in varying seasons, as in the temperate and cold countries. So we lack external cues, except when it rains in the rainy season. But our ancestors were sensitive to this external deficiency and they used to celebrate change of seasons with pompous festivals and a myriad ritual by the calendar. These used to be great events of their life. Were they idle fools who had nothing else to do? No! They also earned for themselves, raised at least five six or more children each as per the prevailing norms and circumstances and lived with no dissatisfaction despite having no Macdonald's or Domino's in their neighborhood. They too valued money and struggled to earn that like we do but that was obviously not their sole pursuit. They also had a taste and an eye for natural happenings. They observed these and enjoyed their days so doing. Are we caught up in a whirlpool of our urban social and economic intricacies and so become mindless of what passes around? Are we in some haste having no time to waste? Has one season and the other only a few degrees of temperature difference to offer?

Go out of your cluttered city and see how it is in autumn there in villages and forest areas. Indira Gandhi would go to Kashmir to enjoy the unique charm that autumn has for its lovers. Same with wintery chills and it's blasts of cold air that pinch deep and one   runs shivering, shrieking and shouting, weeping with pain and laughing with pleasure all at the same time, for life to a warm corner or better still into the arms of your beloved to enjoy. Your hands are cold and the fingers numb and dead while your warm breath blown at them is so comforting. No one gives in to this experience. Instead a great feeling of victory pervades and the heart gets a confidence of having conquered a new realm. It freshens even a morose person. Same with mountaineering. Thousands consider Switzerland more beautiful and worth enjoying in winter than in summer. Mark Twain was in love with snow clad mountain Jungfrau (meaning 'maiden') the highest peak in Switzerland. Read him on the subject and you will agree with me as then. Go and live in a desert for some while all alone or perhaps with someone whom you love and note how it's 'Desertedness', it's all round silence, it's enchanting sky and the warm breeze hypnotize you. Indian city dwellers have never heard the sound of silence. I assure you it is fantastically musical; hypnotizing and rejuvenating. Lend an ear to it please! The heavenly symphony will be audible, if you persist in your efforts. The stars at night are so big and bright and so low in the sky that you may try to touch them with your hand if you have that height of body or perhaps make use of a stool for that. But please never stand on two stools ever. Nothingness 'Shunia' has its own attraction. It can be an experience one will remember all one's life and also learn how to appreciate real beauty. All your worries and stresses of city life are lifted off your shoulders in a jiffy and you feel light and weightless. It may be compared to the experience of weightlessness that cosmonauts enjoy high above. To better explain the situation, I am giving the following two examples:

There was a young lady Mridula, who suffered from cancer of her breast and one breast had already been removed but the disease had spread to the other breast and other body parts also. She was under treatment of our eminent surgeon Dr. SP. Gupta, a friend and mentor to me personally. She was a well-read individual and knew what was going around very well. She had converted to Buddhism; it's mantras gave her solace, she claimed. In that advanced state of her disease I asked her about her pain. She smiled back and asked what any doctor could do for that except making me sleep with morphine which she resented. Sitting on the window sill of her room in the nursing home, which she had strangely made her usual place to sit, she informed me that she found this world intensely beautiful and dear to her, so she sat most of the time on the window watching the flow of activity in the world. She described it as mesmerizing and so avoided being put to sleep by doctors. Mirdula, I realized had little time left and so was in haste to watch and see this world which she thought was enchanting. Was she wrong? Just imagine.

The window of her room in the nursing home did not open on any boulevard or that any modern shopping mall was seen from there nor any public park with its greenery but on an ordinary colony road with cars hurrying to and fro blowing horns in order to push those ahead to run faster and faster. But Mridulla found the scene 'Mesmerizing', as she put it. Why? Mirdulla had remained busy all her thirty years with the mundane run of life as we all are wont to be. She did not have time as well as inclination to witness the real process of this life because she was a part of it then. She was herself in hurry for one reason or the other. Now standing apart from it she appreciated the charm of working of this machine of life; how it's numerous wheels moved and she also heard the myriad sounds that emanated from their working and enjoyed their music as she had never before. Knowing that her time was very short in this world she perhaps felt sorry never to have looked around her with attention and so missed the peculiar charm that is contained even in the din and noise, the hustle and the hurry of our city life and what an average city dweller is usually tired of and wants to run away from.

The other example: In 17th century during the reign of Aurangzeb, **there lived a poet called 'GaniKashmiri'** in some remote village of Kashmir. He wrote poems in Persian language but himself lived as a hermit desiring anonymity for himself and so lived a secluded life. Almost unknown locally he had attained great fame in Iran for his eminent verses and poems. Even Iqbal and Mirza Galib have acknowledged him and the latter is said to have translated some of his verses in to Urdu. It is said that he declined an invitation from Aurangzeb to meet him at Delhi, because he considered all Mughal rulers cruel who exploited the local population. One of his poems wherein he described himself as a lion and owning vast lands and riches had reached the then court poet of Persia who reveled in the verse but could not understand a line or two that had been used. These were no Persian words but Kashmiri words that the poet had inserted under his poetic license to do so. The Persian poet was naturally a rich person but one of some taste for learning also. In his curiosity he travelled from Persia to Kashmir to meet his counterpart and perhaps had hoped to stay in Gani's palace for some time to relax and so dressed in gorgeous costly clothes and wearing chains of gold and pearls round his neck, seated on an elephant, was led to the thatched hut our Kashmiri poet was living in. Opening the door of the hut he was surprised to see Gani sitting on a bare mud floor with a torn 'Pheron' on and so exclaimed 'Is this the one who boasts of being a lion and fabulously rich? Now see the real lion is before you. 'The Kashmiri poet replied 'I do see a lion but it is an artificial one tapestry on a carpet while as here am I, a real jungle lion who owns all the forests around and so am the richest and the happiest one. I maintain these lands and forests as my play grounds. 'The Persian poet was speechless.

The poor poet was happy in his abject poverty because he had the sense to enjoy that poverty also. Had he any use for riches he would have utilized the occasion when Aurangzeb had invited him. As a Muslim scholar of Persian with his fame extending to Persia, the monarch could have bestowed titles, Jagirs and untold wealth on him. But he knew that the main source of man's worries are the same riches after which he hankers day and night. He was a free man describing himself a lion and so he remained to the last. Even now we remember him! Now look at our rich men. Are they happy? Far from that. Worst of all, our middle class too is not happy. They lament their pecuniary position, guided by TV advertisements to purchase more in order to be happy, crave for more and spend their time and energy in acquiring more and more as do our millionaires. And so the rat race! No one has time to pause and enjoy what he has. In reality it does not take money but an aptitude of mind to derive one's happiness. And that needs conscious thought to cultivate that mental state. While Gani was a great intellectual and a poetic mind and needed no outside help to understand the reality of life, our Mridulla was forced to look for her ultimate repose and the intrinsic charm of life, in caged, sad circumstances, in a dull stale scene of a city street. So be careful friends while there is time! Are our millionaires happy? Our illiterate poor villagers are far more so because they live closer to nature.

MONEY DOESNOT BUY JOY: One day I was purchasing vegetables for my home at a vegetable shop and suddenly a neighboring business man reputed in the town(Bhowali) for his wealth also came into the shop and picked up a pumpkin(gourd) asking for its price. In unexpected sarcasm and to every one's surprise there, I exclaimed laughingly 'Hai, do our rich people also eat the same vegetables as we the commoners?' Having heard this unnecessary and irreverent remark the businessman fell silent. His eyes looking at nothing on the floor, his face flushed to reveal a realization of the truth that has evaded all of us so far. I felt discomforted as I saw him looking embarrassed among people who all knew him and perhaps me too. The veg vendor was gleefully laughing at both of us. The rich man slipped out unobserved. Next day I apologized to the rich man at his shop! We are living under a system wherein money alone is supposed to make one happy; reality   of life passes unnoticed. No time for own self!

The other side of the coin; Once I needed change for a five hundred rupee note and tried getting it from the girl sitting at our hospital counter. She told me she had only four hundred rupee notes and I took these, the balance of one hundred remaining with her. After I finished my patients and had to leave, I asked her for my balance. She took it out immediately and handed it over to me, at the same time asking me 'Sir, if I did not pay then what would you do'? She was smiling. My eyes showed anger and I pocketed the note and walked out.

Later it came to me that in our midst even in our so-called middle class, there must be people for whom a hundred rupees is a big sum and perhaps this receptionist was one of them. I felt sorry for my behavior and my stress on our 'so-called' honesty towards such people. Next day I went to her and gave her three hundred rupees. She looked puzzled and asked me 'what for, sir?' I said just to make you happy! She gave a larger smile and looked pleased while attempting to return the money. I pressed it and went my way. Guilt washed clean! American tycoon philanthropy is a trifle?

Far later, I came to know that, that lady's husband suffered from severe depression and was jobless.

Once Prime Minister Vajpayee speaking in parliament on the prevailing corruption, in his eloquent poetic manner one day expressed his wonder as to how much money does a man require to live? Who listened? Fodder, Coal and boforsscamsters were seated in the front rows. What effect and what results?

An anecdote about 'Gani' before we move on: He used to leave the door of his hut wide open when he would go outside but would bolt it from within when he was inside. Asked about this peculiar behavior he replied "when I am out there is nothing costly worth stealing in the hut but when I am inside the hut has high value goods in it. That needs to be guarded."

Now to leave the above topic I am reminded of Sigmund Freud who when asked whom he would describe as a normal person replied 'a person who works well and has a good love (sex) life 'the latter meaning a capacity to enjoy and feel pleased. This includes one's sex life also. While as we will have plenty of occasion to talk about my/our love life/s later, about my work life let me state that I have gradually got transformed into a restless kind, impatient to finish my job. I have also become a slave to my habits. Though with the changes in life that modern times have got in and with more availability of money it has become easy to purchase services I have a habit of doing my things with my own hands as far as I can. This gives me a sense of mastery over my world and an independence of a varied kind. Small and little things of life give me pleasure. Often I remind myself that I am a 'Badshah' a king, a prince because I am not much dependent on others and so remain happy and contented like a real king. I have a purpose in mind while I write this.

BEAUTY: But first, an introduction to some more queer parts of me; details however to wait, till the subsequent chapters are reached. I feel exquisitely happy at the sight of beauty in any of its forms. This is not to say that others don't appreciate beauty. But in my case I have made it a habit imagining the artist himself or his shadow busy at his work and the materials he worked on, for creating his piece of art. Creation of a meaningful and purposeful and above all a beautiful thing ab novo is no small task. Watching it generates an overwhelming feeling wherewith one simply surrenders.

Beauty itself is like a fragrance; yes, it is just fragrance. It is overwhelming; it is enrapturing and spell-binding. It is sheer magic. As smoke at a distance is a sure sign of fire so is beauty a sure sign of brimming life of early years; it is youth at its fullest. Beauty resides in activity, order and system. A flower can be an example. Contrary to common belief, it is on active duty all the while, standing on it's stalk on the plant in the flower bed patiently, swaying with the wind, spreading fragrance and scent and adding to the colours and charm of the garden which has grown and manured and watered it, it is a pleasure, no less a pride for it's gardener. It was born for this purpose to spread happiness and smiles over to onlookers. So it stands on duty active and attractive as long as the stalk bears its weight and the plant continues to supply nourishment. Once asked a master craftsman at tapestry why they drew only blooming smiling and not withered flowers in their designs? Who will purchase that and who likes to look at a crumpled flower, was his answer. Is there any dearth of sadness and misery in the world, he added? Painters in comparison are more welcoming to reality of life but it is hard to find a painting say of roses that also shows the accompanying thorns on the flower-bearing shoot. Seeking joy with no concern for its usual accompaniments of sorrow and pain is naiveté and childishness. Real seekers of joy derive it as much from the flower as from its thorns. Their pricks and scratches are no less dear to them and they cherish that experience. Any love-lorn person will confirm my statement. As a matter of fact, it appears that a beautiful woman, with her myriad attributes, is the actual **materialization of some poet's dream**. Gods with all their artists, designers and sculptors would not, as has been related in mythology, have succeeded in creating this puzzle without a blueprint from a person of delicate tastes and florid imagination. She, no doubt, like many other beauties and charms in life, is an example of near perfection. A really attractive female is that great poet's dream come true. All of us owe him many thanks.

Love in the meadow: Beauty anywhere and in anything is a wonder. A sudden encounter with it makes one realize this. One's eyes become wide open, pupils widen up even in bright light, ears and hearing sharpen up and all senses are suddenly activated, missing a heartbeat may not be unmentionable-all automatic and unconscious work and one is caught unawares at what happens.

Love in Meadow:A long time ago I visited Sonamarg in Kashmir on way to Baltal and onwards, by car. That was my first ever trip there. It was a long drive through dense forests and a massive canal rushing down alongside the road was playing its music all through. Lost to myself in such hypnotizing circumstance, I realized the forest cover was suddenly replaced by a very large open area under a clean blue sunlit sky and I myself was suddenly face to face with a wide unending undulating lush green pasture and grounds. I was breathless and spell bound and dazed for a moment. I couldn't believe my eyes. With my foot on the brake pedal, my hands unclasped from steering I felt my arms involuntarily opening out to embrace the paradise; to put it deep inside me- in my chest somewhere. I had reached Sonamarg! The golden meadow.

Parking the car by the side I crept to the feet of the meadow. Hardly out of the effects of my highway-hypnosis, and now in a daze, I laid myself prostrate on the green grass with my face resting on it while the open palms kept moving to feel it's soothing cool sensation. It felt like newly sprouted and tender or freshly mowed and prepared and dressed for some occasion. And in curiosity I lifted my head to survey the area around to find that the greenery extended to unlimited distances and up to the horizon. Who would mow and dress up such infinite areas and for what occasion or how come the grass had newly sprouted and was so soft and tender in that late-summer season, I puzzled. Had some supernatural hand done it; prepared my beloved in eager loving anticipation of me? Allama Iqbal, one of the greatest poets ever, was correct; she has been waiting for me since ages. Waiting for one who appreciates her charm and beauty, one who loves her deeply from the very core of his being. Has she herself done it, manicured, groomed and laid herself so, to welcome me? Surveying further the area appeared landscaped purposefully with mounds and irregular troughs,highs and lows so placed that the entire area appeared breathing and moving to say something. Looking more attentively, I was surprised to find the round attractive mounds heaving like the breast of a child in sleep. No, I realized; this was my beloved, living and breathing, her breasts heaving at the pleasure she felt on seeing me. A delicate tune from the famed poetess Habbakhatoon ringing in my ears 'this is your garden, come and enjoy, it is already in bloom' now firmly reminded me that she has been waiting for me since long. With her arms open and breasts full and revealing and now full of joy she welcomes me. Tears filled my eyes and I lay once again down to kiss her and to feel her to satisfy my own soul and to calm her heaving breasts. Like a child I frolicked around, shouting with my own self whatever came to me. A never before felt calm prevailed all-round, even the wind had stopped blowing, not even a breeze did move, no birds chirping, no butterflies in the air, the far away forest trees stood silent without a ripple any-where. The mountain sun stood fixed at one place, gazing wide-eyed. Amazed at the 'Leela' that was in progress. It was brighter than ever. It's warmth felt sweet and cool and reassuring in my heart. Were they all stealthily watching in suspense and surprise, with bated breath, the evolving events, that romance of the moment when the mother held her long-separated child in her lap caressing and kissing him and he in turn fondling her riotously, playing pranks to assure himself of her love. The calm and silence around were palpable. Time had slowed it's pace and one could lay a finger over any particular second or even a small fraction of it as it passed by, right in front and around me like a gossamer thin revolving belt carrying a whole baggage of events on to oblivion/eternity. This universe around appeared made of weightless and substance less events; mere flashes of multi-coloured lights projected on to a cinema screen; all and everything moving and changing; apparently as per script. In the final and total this puppet show appeared meaningless but in the immediate appeared coherent and interesting. Just imagine for a moment the possible happenings on this conveyor belt. It pleases like a game of the other to protect their own dear self, strut and fret around for land and power. They at times, appear punny figures. Imagine Alexander the great ordering one of his close friends to be beheaded on spot. No feelings, no mercy no repentance! Indeed, very humane? Perhaps he had got his father king Philip also killed with as much coolness, yet people call him 'gre at'. Timur the lame comes to mind waddling, swaggering and croaking in front of one of his freshly built pyramids of 70000 human skulls to demonstrate his greatness. He considered it his bravery and skill to have murdered 1.5 million mostly unarmed civilians. And that is what passes for greatness in this world? That is the real wonder. Our own Nehru despite the aura of wisdom around him, never uttered a word when, right during his life time, newspapers would daily fill up columns titled 'What after Nehru?'. Obviously he enjoyed and encouraged drumming up the hysteria about his personal greatness. The wiseacre apparently believed that at least India if not the whole world would crumble without his guidance and leadership. It amuses me to think of our many world conquerors, sword in one hand to slaughterothers and shield in the other to protect one's own dear self. And so on with many of those who knowingly strove to appear 'The great'. Where are the tracts and territories they vanquished and where the power they wielded, where the fruit of that wisdom they showered and without which the world would crumble? Strange it is that this picture has neither a fast forward nor a reversing button. Stranger still, that this time-belt visibly slowed it's movement automatically in front of us, perhaps to watch our play and to watch the beauty of the moment. Sensible and live as it obviously is, it must have recorded our tale to be played again and again though with newer actors each time, "in states yet unborn and accents unheard" as the master has rightly put it. Fragrance of peace and love were in the air, permeating everything visible. I felt light-ever light, as weightless as a feather. It was a distance only of a few moments in time when a passionate lusty union of a lover with his long separated beloved in the throes of her youth, make-up and bloom, also took place. Warm blood of youth seeking thrill and excitement, attempting to satiate it's thirst to know her intimately and to taste the merriment of intimacy. Confident of his body and mind and above all in his love he strove to impart that joy and pleasure to his beloved. A union of the universal and eternal with the temporal and evanescent was under way. She cried 'look at my burgeoningcolourful youth and imagine my dreams, Oh the colourful dreams of my throbbing heart'. In joy and happiness, I rolled my body and soul on the green soft grass, kissing it repeatedly, brushing my face over it again and again. I felt relieved. As I said, I felt weightless; all worries gone, entire world forgotten and so skipped around with ease and comfort, as if lifted on wings. O! I was my own self; an emperor in the valley of love, the kingdom of my beloved! A paradise unknown to most.

Flowerygirl: To illustrate the qualities and the sameness of beauty in all it's innumerable shapes and forms, I talk of an identical unexpected but relatively easier to appreciate, sudden happening which occurred one day when I was aged 18 or 19. It concerns a boy and a girl; nothing great, you will say. But I won't agree. Please listen: this affair lasted just a few minutes, perhaps two or three in all. It was intense, so much that it's memory can last as many perhaps two, three or even ten lives and enliven each one of them. It happened near the boundless wilderness of Letpora saffron lands near Pampore in Kashmir. Beauty of the moment, the flavor and the scent in that air, I still savour and feel intoxicated by. But before I relate the matter I must note that such small and little incidents are not uncommon in many people's lives but they are busy in more mundane and often profitable affairs so that flimsy unprofitable events, like seeing fairies pass-by, go unnoticed. Even if noticed, these are also deliberately attempted to be forgotten by neglecting them because these are thought to be below one's dignity or not in keeping with the assumed religiosity and piety of later years. They are also looked down upon as early age foolishness and immaturity and hence not to be talked about by mature and wise grown-ups. So let it be said loudly that such very little incidents are often THE salt of life. They render flavour and richness to it. To realize this fact one must develop a receptive temperament of his own and learn how to recognize niceties of life. Age is no bar to learning anything new and beneficial. One should try to develop a perception for finer qualities of living and feeling,so let me say that I was one-day traveling from Jammu to Srinagar by bus as usual. On way near Pampore our fleet of buses stopped for tea at a road side Dhaba (restaurant) for some time. Restless by temperament that I was, I took a small walk forth to relax myself. Lo! Passing by another bus I saw a beautiful girl of similar age sitting window side in that bus. She looked fresh like a flower. I don't know what happened but words 'Wish I could die for you' in Kashmiri language escaped loud and clear from my mouth. A gleeful smile and wide open happy eyes was

her response to this unexpected sudden unthought of
remark and she bent her head down to hide herself. A
few moments later when I walked back to my bus I
found her watching for me and our eyes met for a while.
Her eyes suddenly reminded me of petals of a lotus
flower. Yes, she was lotus eyed! No talk, no words! She
had heard what my soul had abruptly cried out and now I
realized how her heart responded. It was a moment of
realization. a visionary moment. It was a moment worth
a life time; just joy, joy and thrilling joy only. Joy felt
deep within and all over! I was in the 7th heaven.

The buses left for their destination carrying at least one
restless soul and I like a truly transfixed and mesmerized
lover, kept gazing without even a blink of eye at the
preceding bus all the while till we reached our Srinagar
point. By then my eyes and neck were aching because I
did not let her bus off my sight even for a moment.
Quickly deboarding I ran out to see my flowery one
descend from her bus and now, eagerly and with brimful
expectation I waited and watched all it's passengers
come out but she did not. I felt nervous with a thin
tremor taking hold of my body I got into the bus to
check for myself but she was not there. Had she hidden
herself intentionally to tease me? I just could not find
her! Continuing, I searched and frantically looked for her
in the streets and markets of the city but could not find

her during my entire vacation of 10 to 15 days in Kashmir. Had I mistaken some other bus for her's? Had she got down enroute? I could not accept for my vigilance. Did she fly away? How and where did she go then? Alas, Vanished? Can that be? I ask myself. What happened? Shocking! I stood confused. If anything can choose to be,it can as surely choose not to be! World of heart? Mysterious! Even those that are struck are baffled? What can the uninitiated say? Call it madness. Perhaps true! Perhaps not true? Could it be a rare glimpse of the reality that creates and then sustains us- the ultimate, the infinite sea of love; the source of all beauty and joy in life. (Beauty is truth and truth beauty—Keats; Satyam shivamsunderam) Few, I believe, can imagine the waves of joy and thrill that filled me while I was watching my flowery one. A play of shimmering, restless air bubbles. At the littlest cause-. a sharp, short but sweet pain in the chest, and the show is ended; a delicious dull ache stays as a reminder for the entire life thereafter-cruel?

We have talked much about our happy times so a few sentences about human grief will serve as a relevant contrast. This contrast is somewhat natural but most unfortunate. Sorrow strikes every person in his own way and no two unhappy persons or families resemble. In contrast all happy people are alike happy, difference being in degrees of outward expression. A happy person easily gets friends and companions to join him, the sad man has to seek someone who can listen to his woes and wails. No one, not even the closest can feel the torment and bitterness of sorrow, it's harsh pinch as natively as the actual sufferer does. Others may empathise with the victim but do never experience how it actually cuts and wounds unless perhaps they themselves are struck. Pain of severe depression is said to be more intolerable than that of cancer. Pain of sorrow is bitter and has a cutting, piercing edge. In the realization of these facts, shouldn't one wish those people who cause mass troubles and suffering to themselves face that sorrow and pain? Shouldn't they themselves get a taste of what they are doling to others whole sale? Yes, and they are our power hungry politicians and religious leader's preachers dividing people, man against man, caste against caste and religion against religion for their mean ends. A curse on them! May they each go through a bout of severe depression! That much done, humanity might become relatively peaceful and men happier. I hope.

Going back to our subject: It is a pleasant pastime with fair ones to tease and torment their admirers. Did the flower girl also like all her tribe try that trick? No, I felt sure she was genuine, pure and innocent; she dins' to know the crooked ways of this world. Her smile was

pristine and pure; other worldly, no malice, no mischief.
She would not cheat me; she would never trick me!
Perhaps she was not mortal, the way we are--made of
flesh and blood. She was made of thin mountain air and
that scent of saffron flowers which had already
hypnotized me. Was she? Then it was in her nature to fly
away and that is what she did; never cheated me, never,
never, my love-lorn heart told me! She went as she had
come softly, silently as the gentle breeze, cool and calm
wafting now here now there.; she was too nice! Perhaps
I was napping, dreaming when she flew away. Alas, I
would have seen more of her had I known this. Alas, I
am a dreamer, only a dreamer! Cursed?

Call this a boyish infatuation, love at first sight,
or me a slippery sentimental fool or by any name that
pleases you but one has to agree that beauties of/in life
are all alike, sweet and seductive, stunning yet calm and
innocent looking, cruel yet soothing, compelling yet
elusive. They often dazzle one to blindness for reality.
Yet it is beauty that gives life it's worth and taste. The
butterfly does not dance in the garden for no reason. And
these reasons can be as insubstantial; as the thin air but
of monumental import!

The instance of my flowery girl was definitely a matter
of chance that as is said, can befall anyone but only
fortunate people value such happenings. Besides

drawing-room-vase-flowers and calendar girls, mother nature has strewn invaluable gems and jewels all over: diamonds among stones and gold in sand. The splendid lotus flower grows and remains hidden in mud till you notice it. My flower girl, I can see was no ordinary person. She was I believe, an angel; a whiff of saffron scented air from those fields materialized for one who knew it's value and flew back to her abode in the world of sweet scented saffron, as silently and softly as she had entered. —a vision. One needs eyes to appreciate. Such phenomena, even supernatural as they may appear, these deserve to be valued, remembered and cherished ever as the golden harvest of one's life. These memories add colour to later life. And one feels life not to have gone waste. About my love in the golden meadow, while also being in the lot of lucky ones only, is a matter of mental cultivation and habit formation. One must learn how to fall in love, that is my submission. It pays! Reminiscing past happy and good times and merry experiences is a good habit; recounting them before a company a still better one. It makes everyone happy and one is received by them later any time as an interesting person. Such a one is greeted with a smile-an indication of acceptance and love. No brooding and weeping please. No one, including your close ones, are interested in other's problems and sorrows on a long term basis.

We have talked of female beauty and so may be noted that a really beautiful lady is also a wonder of creation. Only it is more wondrous because it is a walking talking and acting one.Any of it's actions can have multiple and far reaching results. In Urdu there is a poetic/romantic word(none equivalent in English unfortunately) describing her little but meaningful actions called 'Adha', and these resonate in a loveful heart giving meaning to it's throbs and for the lover himself a reason for his sobs.

But we know that all perfection or near perfection is based in a system and all systems have an inbuilt tendency to disorder (entropy of thermodynamics). The more near to perfection the greater the entropy(decay) and so to our sorrow great beauty also does not last long. A beautiful woman like a beautiful flower withers soon to the heart-broken lamentation of all lovers of things attractive. There is a time for every good thing in life. People wait the whole winter to visit gardens and flowery meadows when these are in full bloom and clever people enjoy all bounties of nature at their optimum time. Cleopatra started her hedonistic binge when she was reportedly just sixteen years of age. To her credit she fell only for colourful princes and men of proven charm and halo around them. She knew how to live and later proved that she also knew how to die, die a martyr in pursuit of a pleasurefull life, when she submitted to the 'ader of Nile'.

Beauty in music illustrates the beauty of order and of system in any situation. Music without rhythm is noise and vice versa. Rhythm is the inherent system in music;I t's vibrant life, which renders it beautiful and attractive. In fact whatever appears attractive in this world is because it is based on a system which is strictly followed and gives it it's very existence. To illustrate, it is one thing to look at and appreciate an exquisitely tapestried. rare handmade shawl in a shop window and get transfixed at it's looks but altogether a different experience to watch that craftsman, busy at his needle work, mixing matching, measuring all spontaneously and translating his mental design and feelings into a mesmerizing concrete form of varied shapes and colours. A small stitch marking a round dot or a twig or two of colored thread inserted at appropriate place changes the basic symbolism and meaning of the entire existing picture. It suddenly makes for new unthought of associations and change of meaning in the final creation;a different life is granted to it. It can be an absorbing and enlightening experience. Many people call their car a beauty for it's looks, smooth noiseless dependable and comforting drive. Now stand by the side of your mechanic while he repairs it's engine. (car failures midway were not uncommon in earlier times) It is interesting, informative and you realize the creativeness involved even in such mundane little jobs that concern your life. It is not the nut or the bolt or a new twig of wire that replaced an old part but the reestablishment of that missing link in a system that has given back the car it's new life. It's beauty lives in a beautiful system which had broken down-a link somewhere. Precious gems and rare arts and exhibition pieces scattered randomly in a room make that place fit for a rich lunatic but arranged systematically and placed in order, the same make that room worthy of royalty. One has, however, to be a little imaginative. Try and look, say, at a portrait of Mona Lisa and imagine the master creator while he painted to create her. It is sheer amazement. The last swipe of a painter's brush can change the very sense of what he had drawn thus far. He has completed the link between his thought and his creation. It is now a meaningful live system. I surmise that the enigmatic smile on the face of monalisa is the work of the last finishing touches by the artist; the final swipes of his brush that puzzle the world unto this day.

A scientist's research and his laboratories appear small and petty in comparison then. While as the latter mostly discover what stands already created, the artist's hands create and give birth to what might be unimaginable even for that scientist. Sight or a mere mental reflection of a sculptural or painted master piece, or a strand of musical composition transports a person into an altogether different world, a world of peace and serenity and love only. There is no place for quarrels, and killings in it. Even the concepts of space, time, gravity etc. etc. of our scientist lose their meaning and significance. Shadows and images of great artists, writer creators and thinkers busy in their work, often become visible to one's mind in such situations and one bows in gratitude. Please don't think you are reading a schizophrenic's rambling. On the contrary, when I think for example of our world, I wonder, why did' not men like Einstein and Stephen Hawking turn mad (god forbid) at the sheer beauty, immensity, perfection and the clock work precision of this universe, after they conceived it in their mind's eye? The initial birth and Construction and later it's evolution and working of this our universe and it's smallest bits is art at it's infinite mark as one feels it and it's very conception must be overwhelming. Inconceivable amounts of energy and forces that are unleashed and their play according to set rules are the ingredients used in this art form. The colours and sounds that must accompany such an extreme happening defy ordinary conception. It'sgorgeosity and glory and majesty and the vastness of accompanying fireworks and illumination; I wish we could imagine; the joviality of the moment. Can a better canvas be ever painted? Not an iota of any shadow, no darkness. Only infinite brightness and shiny kaleidoscopiccolours in the sky, meteors and falling stars circling whizzing past, whistling joy and surprise in ears; just imagine please! That is how birth of this universe was celebrated. Our books on physics and astronomy give only half the truth about the birth of our world. They don't tell us that it was a grand carnival of lights, colours and music, glorious in every way! I don't suppose we will be criticized too much for saying so. Because it is after all a matter of looking at an event from a different angle; how one takes it. What is called the big bang, I call 'the great grand bang'. Everything about it was great and grand. A thousand musicians in the orchestra playing celestial tunes and a thousand guns booming in salute with all heavenly lights of a myriad colours flashing. Never seen and never known-before fireworks blazing in the sky, all in concert. Holi and Diwali, two in one! Jubilant Gods, enjoying? Som-rasa (divine drink) and Bhang are really effective! We ought to have been invited to the spectacle. Do Gods lack courtesy?

Just imagine if Einstein instead of being a physicist were a poet, would we be having another Shakespeare, Kalidasa or Ghalib with us now? In place of arithmetical equations and geometrical squares, circles and arrows representing magnetic and gravitational forces handed down to posterity and which the common man will never understand, hitherto unknown blossoms of joy and ecstasy created out of new found rhythms and waves of magical words and lyrics would perhaps have enriched humanity no less. With every word a pearl and every verse an invaluable neckless, our world would have been far more interesting. And how unfortunate as much as reflecting the mental poverty of our race, we have not been able to produce a single Shakespeare over past 400 years plus. This is not to belittle Einstein but to praise him. He was one of our greatest. But poets are ever known to be greater than the greatest. See how 'Gani' poet rejected emperor Aurangzeb's invitation to visit him. He called him a cruel king because of his open suppression of Hindus.He knew the truth. What could have that 'poor emperor' given him? Gani lived in majesty and already possessed everything! Kings and emperors wearing crowns and coronets come and go, swept away by the winds of time like dust in the street outside, but royalty of the poet is immortal and everlasting and ever overpowering. What is more, the poet has the power to confer greatness and even immortality on others too, on whomsoever he chooses.

Poets are the greatest of Men
Julius Caesar, with all the faults of the then Romans, was perhaps just an armed chieftain, fighting and

quarreling for ascendancy with many others like him, chiefly against Pompey. History books would have reserved at best a passing sentence or a paragraph for him like for other Roman generals and Kings. He stood nowhere in comparison as a great and virtuous man or a ruler to say, our Shivaji Maratha, Rana Partap, Rani of Jhansi or even the all virtuous King Zainul-allabudin(Budshah) of Kashmir. Great kings and emperors in history like Chandragupta maurya, Ashoka, Akbar, Darius, Xeresis of Persia or Salaudin of Egypt would feel insulted if compared to him. **Yet Shakespeare made him one of the greatest of this earth and also immortal to the very end of human remembrance.** The poet-dramatist was so confident of his powers that he declared 'In states yet unborn and in accents and languages yet unknown' will Julius Caesar be remembered and praised; just because the poet chose it so. It is he who put the words 'For I am Caesar' in his mouth and described and decorated him so as to be fit to utter these grandiloquent words and other famous dialogues that are the pride and pleasure of English language for all time to come. We forget that the play was written 450 years afte caesar's death and that language and dialogues used are fit only for stage setting.Any body howsoever great and mighty he may be will be taken for a mad megalomanic if he talks in this dramatic prose in his daily life, and not respected and loved as Caesar is reputed to have been.It is the playwrite's magic which compels us to believe a living Caesar and other personae,in flesh and blood uttering the words reserved for them. In odder that you don't laugh at me for my above statement about Julius Caesar please remember Brutus in this regard.

 Who was Brutus in real life? A garden variety Roman aristocrat and money lender who like all their nobles lived on the blood and sweat of slaves and plebeians. He lent money on interest @ 40% and when not paid back would send forces to expropriate the same. Yet our poet has chosen to make him an example republican, perhaps even a democrat full of all virtues of sympathy and love for the common masses and a hatred for oligarchy and despotic autocracy. No one can question the poet. It was his sweet will, license and prerogative to say whatever he chose to say. He was/is greater than the greatest and we bow our heads. Likewise, Ganiinvigorates us even today. The thunderous applause and clapping his verses evoked in Iranian court 200+ years ago are still ringing in our ears. Again, was there never a woman as beautiful as Cleopatra born before or after her? But Cleopatra's beauty is extolled by Shakespare sky high and that remains in his power to do.It is his greatness and the magic and the beauty of his words, not the (wanton) lady's, that compels us to think of her as we do Think for a while on the words "She makes hungry where she satisfies the most" .Can anyone improve upon this declaration on female beauty? Final and ultimate has been said in these eight words! And that is what a poet or a great artist has the power and unrestricted liberty to do or undo. No emperor, president or prime minister can question or object!

And now the day to day running, no less the complexity and scale of this universe. It is simply mystifying, breath taking! But how and why was it made? How it was made, we can with our present knowledge of physics and chemistry almost surmise. **But why it was made nobody knows.**<u>But I have an answer! Don't please call it a mad man's reply</u>. This beautiful universe was definitely made for me; and you too perhaps. I said perhaps because if you don't care to look towards it, then it is not meant for you.

A SUGGESTION;whenever you go out for an excursion to a hill station, try go into the nearby jungle. In a clearing amongst the pines spread a bed sheet on the grass and lie down face towards the sky. Now watch the sky and the surrounding tree tops. You are used to looking at the world from up- downwards, today you are seeing it down- upwards. Relax a little, you will realise how the trees and the sky are looking back at you. They were waiting for you. Now remember Dr. Iqbal' s verse about Nargis (given in page 42,). This verse will be the

'Mantra' for your peace of mind now on. So keep repeating it in your mind and understand it's deep meaning and deeper significance well. Take deep breaths of the nimble air around you. After some time when you get up to go you will feel some change in yourself. Please repeat this process for a few days and if nature(Prakriti) accepts your love for her, you will find a breeze blowing one day and the trees dancing, swaying their tops in joy and the wind is creating music while flowing through the dancing pines who are keeping time with this symphony. While you were busy enjoying the dance of pines you missed seeing the blue sky. It was stealthily peeping at you through the leaves, smiling. Happy at the evolving love story(Lila). You will never forget this incident; will keep pinning for it. You will remember the incident often back home and will seek it again and again in multiform settings and places. You are in love! And lo, your comprehension and thinking about our universe has changed. Perhaps you are a little happier and contended also. Goethe has rightly said 'Life is grey but nature is green'. Please find time to know that green; it will fill you with joy!

It is our great luck to be a part of this wonderful drama as it unfolds itself in our life. But one question has ever intrigued me. When we talk of natural beauty, does it not include beauty of our females too? Who has made them whatever they are? It is a curse of the human mind to separate human beauty from what is called natural. We have an explanation for this queer human behavior in psychoanalysis. We have a sense of guilt about our sex dating back to the dawn of civilization and so we don't want anyone to know that we are perpetually thinking about our opposite gender. This mentality has been reinforced by our religions by associating a sense of sin with all forms of sexual thinking and behavior, even of marital sex (Read St. Paul).Some Muslims still subject their women to clitoral circumcision (Mutilation) so that they should not enjoy any pleasure/attraction in coitus; pleasure being sinful (for ladies).Such women behave like soft bags filled with cotton, never having been allowed to know the reality of joy in intimate companionship. They are only meant to produce children, by the dozen like rabbits and pigs; to increase the population of the faithful. Allah is happy!

In fact human beauty and charm are one of the highest and the most noble of nature's creations, reaching it's zenith in female beauty A poet calls ladies 'Pareizada' (same genus as fairies). That itch to get attracted to beauty which I call 'Love Itch' is a universal phenomenon, only it's expression varies in different individuals. Artists and people of a poetic, easy going temperament and like me, restless radarless types are candidates who value or even overvalue their experience in the field and cherish "the harvest of glorious memories" all their life. I am perhaps a dreamer over much; no harm intended or done. Here, as a short forenote, I relate it's first teething or blooming of this instinct in me with the following incident which I naturally consider important and hence worthy of mention:

My own youth, as is the case with youngest men was, I consider, quite colourful but innocence was it's hallmark unlike what is seen these days. I remember the first time I had occasion to talk to an unknown girl on the road. That was obviously a milestone in my life's course. I was in my 12th year at college which was a large co-educational institution but I was shy of girls and never attempted to talk to any female class mates. One morning, however, I left my residence for college but found no other students with book bags going that way which would normally be full of students both male and female at that hour. Soon however I spotted a lone girl student among the walking public ahead of me and more in order to take a chance to talk to her than to find out facts I hastened my pace and on reaching near her made bold to address her. 'Are we alone going to college today' I muttered partly breathless and mostly nervous and shaking. I was smiling an artificial forced smile. Her head, covered with a shawl turned to me and she looked surprised. I could discern nervousness in her looks and talk also when she too replied me briefly with a forced smile in a faint voice, 'It seems so'. But what happened to the usual throngs, I encouraged and pushed myself to ask. Now I was positively breathless and my words poured out haltingly. I was feeling embarrassed also. She was kind and dismissed me with a slight shake of her head. Perhaps she was equally frightened; testing wings like a new hatched bird. It had been declared a holiday by the Govt on the radio but we two did not know that. But this experience gave me courage nonetheless, to face girls in the following times and I started considering myself as an experienced man in matters of love not knowing then what hazards fate had in store for me in future. So I was happy and remember it to this day. Hands on job experience! I can see that everybody is happy when he tastes of the opposite gender even from a distance, as I did but the road ahead can be dangerous; hazards in flight! Somehow I went along and the wreckage/salvage is for you to examine and take lessons from. In the medical college, I imagined myself, perhaps the most handsome boy at least in the hostel, nay the whole college and assumed appropriate airs. To add to this our Principal would hail me, every time I met him, as a great swimmer from Kashmir because I had noted in the application form for admission that I had crossed Dal lake to and fro, a distance of two and a half to three

miles then. Now, please forgive me and allow me to go
back to where we left talking of my work-mania etc.

Chapter V

<u>A DOCTOR SPEAKS</u>

Before I open other miscellaneous accounts I must do a little doctoring-my profession. (It's application in present context will be known and is explained in last chapter under caption 'Aim of life'). To this end I propose to start it as follows:

SELF HELP;So let us take the little case of plumbing your leaking kitchen tap for example or righting a dysfunctional electric bedroom switch; imagine the great sense of achievement it generates in oneself. It is euphoric, no less than what Alexander the great must have got with each of his conquests. I have developed a habit of attending to minor home repairs myself. These consume some idle time of mine, get me busy and generate a sense of mastery and confidence in me. Often a feeling of independence too. I feel myself more complete after every such conquest. Anyone who has never tried his hand at such self-help may perhaps laugh at what is said. The more complicated the job the greater the delight at it's accomplishment. Dignity of labour is also implied. People who use their hands for physical or mechanical work develop the small muscles of their hands well; their coordination and dexterity gets developed and clumsiness reduced. This is an important aspect of brain's work. Mental function is strengthened along with your hand improvement. Complexity and the degree of refinement achieved in the working of hands differentiates humans from lower species. Working of the thumb, it's versatility and range of movement in particular appears to be related to human brain development.

This is not to boast but certainly with some sense of pride that I must relate that I do all my cleaning washing and maintenance of my little clinic, guest room and our living room myself. This plus my morning schedule of exercise takes me some 2 hours or more every day and gives me much satisfaction. I detest going in a man driven rickshaw and often have got down from it to run beside it whenever chance compels me to hire one for the sake of my wife. Lo! How virtuous and angelic I am? Wait a moment my friend, I will tell you my misdeeds and you will recognize the monster who is praising himself so. A small one comes to my mind now but more may come later! Once I stole Rs.156/- or so the amount was, from a patient of mine. It was in 1970s and this sum mattered then. A person comes to a doctor for relief of his suffering and the doctor steals money from him; unpardonable! I plead, I have some extenuating circumstances to advance in my defence but will detail those later. ("Sale price of a doctor") So don't call me a little devil that soon. For the present to go back to my presentable self I must say that morning exercise and household work has become my habit and a life pattern. I feel out of sorts when for any reason I am deprived of this - my morning chore.

WEAKNESS OF MEMORY; STANDING ON HEAD EXERCISE-Our life and work styles have lately involved an increased emphasis on intellectual and memory functions of our brain and there are an increasing number of people who complain of problems in these areas. Let me say that there are no medicines known that can improve our memory or intellectual functions and so let us not be cheated. One must, on the other hand try to retain one's natural mental powers by methods other than purely medical. Once organic changes in brain set in, these cannot be reversed; stress has to be on their prevention. Hence I have decided to make a special mention of the exercise of 'Standing on one's head- 'ShirshAsan' because I believe that it positively helps and also because this is practically neglected by our yoga teachers in general, to the detriment of general public. I am also giving some suggestions about how to easily start doing this exercise which may otherwise appear difficult and even dangerous to adult and senior starters. This too forms a part of my exercise routine. This I have restarted after a long pause. I am 78 years of age and had lately started forgetting names of medicines which I prescribe to my patients. In fact forgetting names of people has been an old malady with me. But forgetting medicine names I thought would affect my clinical practice and so my livelihood. So I restarted Shirshasan. It has been nearly 2 years since and I do it for nearly 10 minutes daily and must report my betterment of memory. I feel agile and active mentally after every session. My memory improvement can also be a false feeling- just part of a psychological feeling of wellbeing but I am observing myself attentively and believe the Asana has helped me materially. Could this be due to an improved circulation of the head and brain, I wonder. The whole column of blood in the body stands full weight and pressure on a tiny cerebral vascular bed perhaps helping it open up a little. The smaller arteries inside the brain are hair breadth wide vessels wherein a dilatation of a few microns can obviously make a difference. Could this help in retarding the age related damages including cerebral atherosclerosis, (fatty deposits within small blood vessel causing their narrowing) God knows! After all why don't our legs and arms have narrowing and atherosclerotic complication as often, except in some recognized diseases like Berger's and Reynold's. This is a personal opinion and no scientific proof is claimed. I relate a personal experience here: I had been prescribed a medicine for my eyes several months ago and having stopped it for nearly 2 months now I wanted to restart it but found that I had forgotten it's name. Similarly, I had seen a picture of a beautiful Swiss- lake called Interleukin on a wall calendar long ago and had forgotten that name too. Recently I was trying hard to remember these two names but without success and suddenly while doing my head-standing exercise 2 days ago both these names cropped up in my mind, only I was not sure about the use of letter 'K' in the lake's name and had to check it on the internet to find myself right in choosing the letter in place of letter 'C'. I don't know how to explain this sudden remembrance during the exercise.

Forgetting is often complained of by young working people and this arises primarily either from mental distractions due to tensions or because the individual is not interested in the job and would unconsciously wish to forget about the disliked project. Students often forget disliked subjects. Forgetfulness before the age of 55 to 65 is nonorganic and purely psychological in nature, and yet another cause of tension and hence adds to the original complaint. This only needs some little treatment and advice.True Alzheimer's is a type of dementia that occurs around ages of 55 to 65 years(pre-senile years)In contrast forgetfulness of old age is a normal process like the greying of hair and has to be accepted as such; there is no treatment for this or for Alzheimer's. Perhaps Shirsh asana may help, as explained. But doctors will do well never to prescribe ACEIs like donepzil, mimentine etc. These are useless-totally. And now we switch back:

I must state that the purpose of my going into description of exercises for brain and heart and lungs etc. is because one's physical health and in particular that of brain is absolutely necessary in order to be able to 'feel' and enjoy the taste of life, as I am attempting to explain. It'sultimate purpose will become clearer as we talk about the 'Aim of life', in the last chapter.

Going further a little, one has to remember that our heart, lungs and the rest of circulatory apparatus form one complex system acting and reacting with the brain through neuronal, hormonal and circulatory regulatory connections making that an equally intrinsic part of their working. Health or disease of one part are sooner or later reflected in the other parts. It can accordingly be said that a well exercised breathing system will help the heart and it's vessels to stay healthy and prevent heart attacks while keeping the brain well-nourished and oxygenated. Various forms of Pranayama (**Breathing exercises**) accordingly form the easiest route to good health. Remember over- breathing and panting during your jogging or running is a tonic for all the three parts of this system in a healthy individual so should be encouraged and not be afraid of.

Shirsh asana as has been told above can be of special use to patients of bad lungs, like in chronic bronchitis and breathlessness. In that case it should preferably be preceded by a short session of steam inhalation for 3 to 5 minutes to soften the outpourings of respiratory passage so that these drain out easily upon tilting your body, head down and trunk up. (Postural drainage).

I am myself a patient of hypertension (high blood pressure) and on drugs for that. I have nevertheless found that episodic break through and fluctuations of B.P occur commonly in high B.P. patients as in me. I have found breathing exercises (Pranyama) help control these within minutes. You may try it out yourself if needed. Simply take a really deep breath filling your chest to the maximum with air. Now close your mouth and nostrils with your hand for 10 seconds and then exhale the breath completely using a bit of force to empty your lungs completely, as much as you can so that your chest shrinks in a little as does your abdomen. Wait for a short while say 5 to 10 seconds again and then inhale again fully. Repeat this full inbreathing and full out breathing at least 5 times. Wait for a minute or two and check your B.P. It has gone down considerably and your head ache etc. if any has vanished.

The above breathing exercise if coupled with Vulselvamanoeuvre viz., holding one's breath and forcing it down into your chest towards the belly, done a few times any time of the day can help patients of palpitations and fast pulse. This exercise helps vagus (a nerve controlling heart beats) nerve to retain some predominance so that irregular heartbeats and even fast irregular beats (Fibrillation etc.) in predisposal people may perhaps be prevented. In fact if one has clinically to differentiate between a serious irregularities of heart from non-serious (functional) one, the easiest way is to take a few deep breaths and force these down your chest while you hold your breath. Stoppage of irregular heartbeats by so doing proves them as harmless 'extra-systoles' caused often by anxiety, excess tea or coffee, smoking etc.

Forced deep breathing (repeated daily vulselva) may help prevent coronary (heart) attacks, I believe. An air filled turgid left lung, in this exercise, keeps gently massaging the left and front surfaces of heart which contain the more important blood vessels called 'left coronary and circumflex vessels, and so should prevent their hardening and closure, as cause a heart attack (More in last chapter.)

Shirsh asana, if any one desires to start must be done v. cautiously in case of grown up and aged people for fear of injury to one's neck or fall. But children of all ages should be encouraged to learn it, I believe. Nehru did it daily, he writes. Late starters, if they desire starting this exercise of standing on head may start with the following method:

LEARNING SHIRSH ASANA; Stand about 2 to 3 feet away from a wall with your back towards it and bend your body into an inverted V so that your head supported by two hands touches the ground while the toes of your feet support your legs; the hips forming the top of inverted V stand in the air. Please practice this much of the Asana for as long as you can upto a maximum of 10 minutes daily. For the elderly even this much of the exercise should be sufficient and will soon prove valuable. They need not proceed any further than this 'supported asana'.However, if continued so, you will soon find that your inanimate wall will come to love you very soon for your persistence and so will encourage you to raise your feet and their toes on to it in a creep and afford a satisfaction of a full shirsh asana to you without having to suspend your legs in the air unsupported. Very elderly and weak individuals may modify the asana as follows: Lie on your bed face down and protrude your head and arms including shoulders from one side of the bed. Now lower these exposed parts of body as much as you can do comfortably and support yourself by two hands on the ground. This forms a transverse L with it'sshort arm supported on ground. Please stay in this head lowered position for as many minutes as is comfortable. Take deep breaths all the while. These perhaps pump waves of blood at varying pressure into the lowered head and should be beneficial.

 Punch line: Henry Ford when asked about exercise remarked "Exercise is bunk. When you are well you don't need it and once ill you can't take it". He died 79. Mr. Ford's demise reminds me of **DEATH AND IT'S FEAR;** a common subject seldom discussed (because it evokes fear even in dreams) but lurking in every mind just beneath the surface. Now, let us remember that death comes when it has to; there is no treatment for that. It is however debatable if exercise or yoga or anything else can prevent or delay death. It is usually multifactorial and hence no statistical analysis or study can reveal effects of exercise or even treatment given for it.TV advertisements recommending a particular edible oil or Atta or even the western trend of adopting the so called Mediterranean foods like olive and it's oil are nonsense, to say the least. These foods and oils etc. are meant for the gullible and those fools who have got money. Drugs meant to reduce blood cholesterol are perhaps no better in ultimate effect. In my view there are only two animals who can develop high blood cholesterol and fats. These are no. 1. Well-fed, unexercised Humans and no. 2. Pet dogs who are fed well but kept tethered or caged in the kennel and so without any walking. Cows in dairy sheds would also get it but for their milk production which reduces their fats automatically and their vegetable diet. Without making any direct comment about the cholesterol reducing drugs prescribed by doctors to each and every one who complains of pain in chest or has high BP. I would recommend regular brisk walking for at least 35 minutes every day. Try to avoid cholesterol reducing drugs as much as you can, please. Nobody knows their long term after- effects yet. Most modern drugs act at sub-cellular enzymatic levels and it is hard to predict their effects at the gene level. They may cause genetic mutation to reveal their effects in your progeny if not on yourself.

A bit of diversion again: Why are people afraid of death? Is it because it is thought to be painful? But pain is associated not with death per se but the disease that can cause death like in cancer, etc. Many deaths are essentially painless and most diseases that because death are not accompanied by unbearable pain and suffering. Heart attacks are known for the deaths they cause and not for pain. Pain of a heart attack is completely relieved either by drugs or by death. Many dying men don't even know that they are dying and some keep making plans for future even on their death beds, some die in sleep, and so on. It is possible that those who die in sleep perhaps feel a sense of suffocation from a failing cardio-respiratory apparatus for some while or a sinking feeling in the chest due to irregular beating of heart etc. and so wake up for a small time and only to loose consciousness due to failure of blood to reach their brain. A conscious person suffering from suffocation or sinking in his chest, if he gets the time will seek relief for his suffering first and thereafter will ask for prevention of his death. I know of a rich man who was ailing for many days and kept ordering his many sons about their business right up to the final moment, when he gasped for breath and then lay motionless. He suffered from a long continued fever and so had no pains. For those who die of sheer ageing it is mostly a silent end. People dying in accidents don't think or worry about death but are actively crying for relief of their pain till they finally collapse. Any person who fears imminent death while in full consciousness and with no apparent cause has a psychiatric disease.

INCAPACITATING ILLNESS; A common question asked is whether people suffering from long continued incapacitating illness like paralysis, especially in old age feel their suffering or pains. Is that a miserable life? The answer perhaps is a 'No'. A damaged brain either due to any major hemorrhage or thrombosis or severe injury or for that matter advanced dementia, will not retain enough power or capacity for discrimination of elaborate sensations. Some elementary kind of pain/pleasure sensation may be regained after the initial trauma/shock is over but real sensations and their pinch is only felt with time as recovery proceeds. In cases where the situation remains unimproved the patient despite having regained consciousness, is not usually conscious of his actual state. He may utter an occasional grunt or even some word/s but these are usually involuntary acts without much substance. So what seems miserable and agonising to onlookers and attendants may not be so for the patient himself. He himself could be far beyond what we call 'miserable'. Unconcerned? Old people to take things easy; let the children have a chance to serve you. In any case you won't know much about that and even may be no worse if not taken care of. Uncared brain damaged patients don't last long. They soon merge with eternal bliss. So be brave!

To continue with our subject; could fear of death be related to a fear of eviction from this world where you have spent so much time building relations, love and affection, caring for many and in turn being cared for by many whom you would like to help or at least to see them doing well; your likes and dislikes, and so on but not in the least for a fear of losing what you possess and that which has taken so much of your effort and time to make and for which you had many plans. Death threatens to destroy all our cherished hopes and aspirations. It is perhaps a little like being suddenly evicted from your house without any notice. The house which you had owned and known to be absolutely yours for 50, 60, or 70 years and could do anything with it, is threatened to be taken away from your hands. Under normal conditions we can't imagine such a situation arising but if one dwells deep into it one realizes how frightening the matter can be. The matter becomes immensely shocking and catastrophic if you are apt to be evicted from your entire world. A threat of a prison sentence turns anybody pale because it implies a forcible eviction from your home/your little world on to a jail. In grown up and elderly people the fate of their progeny is a cause of grave concern. It is stated that prophet Abraham did not agree to die till he was assured by God that his descendants will prosper well in Cannan. In any case elderly people and even middle aged ones fear prolonged disability like a paralysis and physical dependence on others more than death. In fact many people are heard praying for death while their limbs are functioning.

It is interesting to note that very young children, perhaps uptill age of 4 to 5 years consider someone else's death like the deceased having gone away somewhere and the reasons for that are also very different from adult reasoning. There is no sense of fear attached to that 'going away', in the child's mind. Fear of death as the adults know it, is an acquisition of subsequent years. Now he fears his own death also as the growing years bring along a growth of relationships, childish hopes and aspirations, sense of ownership etc.

In the final may we conclude that fear of death attributed to fear of pain that accompanies it may not be correct. It is actually a fear of being forcibly evicted from this dear world of oar's that is the real reason behind fear of death. Fear of painful diseases in particular cancer is quite prevalent in the population but forms a separate subcategory. My conclusions are obviously challengeable, but I have consulted several leading authors around this subject but have found no convincing answer.

NEAR DEATH EXPERIENCE; May I here write about **a personal experience** relating to the above subject: It is some twenty years ago that one day as usual I went to our toilet to pass urine. I had not bolted the door of the bath. And Lo, I was found lying fully unconscious on the floor of the place by my wife who in desperation had called in our neighbors and when I woke up I found to my surprise two neighborhood doctors checking me up; an ECG machine had been set up and so on. This happened when I was quite healthy ad fit physically in every respect and I was proud of my health. It was a common form of syncope(unconsciousness) called a 'Micturition syncope' and was confirmed so on investigations proving me physically alright. This syncope can happen to anyone after he empties his urinary bladder in a standing position or when he stands up suddenly from his squatting posture. This is obviously no matter to talk about. What I want to say is about what I felt during that spell.

I was perhaps not fully unconscious at least in the beginning and I distinctly remember my feelings and thinking then.I did feel myself stooping with my head drooping low on my shoulders somewhere and there appeared to me a small collection of water on the floor and this was very near my low lying face. Suddenly it came to me "was I dying?" But I found that sensation of dying or whatever that was, quite delicious and I remember lowering my head intentionally a little more to increase that sensation saying to myself "Then let it go on and let me die. "I had no concern then about the world or my wife or children and above all of myself as well. It was somehow sweet.

Whether someone else accepts my description as is given above or not or whether my experience was correct or not, I have derived a belief from this my experience that dying in itself is not painful as is usually thought. On the contrary the experience may be delightful. This naturally does not include the suffering or pains that the disease causing one's death may involve. Who after all can say that cancer pains before one's death are delightful. It is obvious even normally that it is one's consciousness only that gives us our sensitivity for pain and suffering and even our sense of pleasure. But dulling of consciousness like with injections of morphine, relieves our sensations of pain and suffering while at the same time releasing some feelings of innate happiness and oblivion and unconcern with our day to day life. No wonder that people seek it in wine and cocaine and other drugs. Dying after a disease of some duration may offer some relief also.It will lengthen our description to explain that the horizon of our worldly interests gets gradually narrowed with advancing years and at one's death bed one's perception and concerns are minimal and it is almost a tubular view of the world that a dying man has. It is an inbuilt mental defense mechanism to reduce one's pain and suffering and this nervous bloc works in direct proportion to the intensity of a man's agony. At the maximum of agony, in acute states, the system gets overloaded and circuits, so to say, get automatically cut off and the man passes into shock, either neurogenic or psychogenic, thereby saving him from excessive pain or suffering. In chronic ailments of vital organs like the heart, lungs or kidneys liver etc. one's consciousness of environment keeps diminishing in direct proportion to the progress of the disease due to it's effects on the brain. So let us not be that afraid of death unless of course you have billions and want to spend them yourself. I can assure you that the tubular view of world as explained will leave you unconcerned about those billions also. Even otherwise also, those billions become useless once a person gets struck by a serious disease. Who wouldn't exchange all his riches to set right his paralytic limb, but those riches are useless then. In a case, death that is perceived by the fully functional mind (an average healthy person) as frightening and painful may actually not be so because of the defence mechanisms in -built in our system as explained. Hence one may as well not think of death so long it does not catch one in reality. And then at that moment you will be incapable of thinking about it or like me, if you feel it pleasurable may actually welcome it as given about my personal experience earlier. While the dying man is, according to our conclusion, untroubled by his onrushing death, those that surround him then or hear of his death later, feel fearful of it because they empathize with his state of existence at that moment.

They are filled with pity as they are reminded of their own possible death and hence feel terrible about it. Accordingly, death gets a bad name and advertisement in the population more so when a young person dies. In that case every one unconsciously argues with his self 'If death could take this young man, what about me.' Hence the general horror.

Even at the cost of being thought wrong, I would compare dying to a pebble falling into a pond. It falls with a splash and sinks but raises ripples in the water which are seen by the onlookers. The bigger the pebble greater the splash and more the ripples and waves. The onlookers and sympathizers fear a similar fate for themselves; a total oblivion and hence are distressed and horrified. In any case we will have to await confirmation of our suppositions till some trustworthy man communicates about his own experience following his death. Till then let us assume that it is a matter of a slight splash and a few ripples that frighten us.

Going back to Shirsh Asana, I remember my Head master Saifi sahib for having taught us this magnificent thing. He was a Kashmiri Muslim of impeccable character and description and like most Kashmiri Muslims of that time never cared about other's religion. That generation of Muslims was, I assure you completely different from the present fanatic rabble. Our

Muslim teachers like their Hindu colleagues commanded love and respect from all. Saifi sahib would himself go 'walking' round our school ground on his hands; standing on head motionless was no feat for him. He did so in order to attract us to the art and to encourage us. Another of our head masters whom I remember was Iqbal sahib. He was very particular about our English pronunciation and exhorted us to listen to BBC English news bulletins for that. Such were our old Govt. school teachers both Hindus and Muslims. They were living examples for their students to follow; real great men. My heart opens up whenever I think or talk about our Kashmiri Muslims. They were completely different from their coreligionists in rest of India and from the Allah-wale (God's men) maulvis who were sent there from U.P. madrasas to preach religious intolerance and hatred of Hindus to new generations. The more religious out of them were the more tolerant and more kind towards other religious groups. They respected Kashmiri Pandits and we loved them; Wahabi fanaticism and hatred was unknown. We trusted them and felt our life and honour safe with them. But, alas, the U.P. madrasas came out victors; Kashmiris with their gentle forefather's blood in their veins got changed; their minds were poisoned.

For a change now, let the doctor speak of his **SALE PRICE:**

One day, long ago I was escorted by a group of 3 or 4 people in an open jeep to a suburb of our city to see a patient. It was a mid-summer day and the weather pleasant; the breeze in the open jeep seductive and soothing. We reached a house located amidst afruit orchard which was bisected by the private drive way nearly three quarters of a mile long. The house looked large but average externally. But as we entered I was amazed at it's internal glamour, it's marble floored long and distant looking corridor, the coloured marble going up it's high laid walls; a queue of huge chandeliers glowing the ceiling a dull golden yellow; the place had a palatial aura. Men's body height appeared getting reduced, at least mine did feel so to me, as we proceeded till an extra sized door went open and I was ushered in to a bed room. It was dark inside the room but as the curtains were raised I felt myself in the center of a film shooting set of the famous film 'MugleAzam'. It was glamorous! Through the full glazed window wherefrom curtains had just gone off, waters of a lake were shimmering in the sun and I imagined that things could be nobetter in any bungalow on the banks of lakeInterleukin in Switzerland. I was feeling giddy! Puzzled at which Maharaja or Maharani was I expected to see and treat. My enigma!

Soon my eyes went round to find a diminutive figure of a woman seated on a bed in the middle of this oversized room. She was dressed in black mostly as per the custom among Muslim ladies in the place. Nothing outstanding in those outstanding environs. And Lo! I recognize the lady as an old patient of mine who came to my clinic almost weekly sat on the wooden bench outside uncomplaining, waiting for her turn and then paid me my humble fee of 20 rupees for the consultation and went away as silently. I cried out,' Could you be our Fa......' and her head nodded in affirmation. I felt relieved. And then I talked to her at my ease, handed over a prescription to a man standing by and walked out after a cup of tea.

At the gate outside a group of men received me back and the person at the head took out a bundle of notes (don't remember the denomination, but most were big notes) held them open in his two palms to say "doctor your fees". He naturally knew my petty fees which his wife had been paying me every week and I felt confused at the sight of this offer. I felt smaller now,a pygmy in presence of a super-rich Maharaja. Had I wasted my life so far? What cost my training and education? and what it's sale price? A strained effort; a hesitant unsure voice from my throat replied "pay me two hundred". It was done; price paid I was dispatched back in the same jeep.

Nearly ten days later the same gentleman reported along the patient to my clinic. I had by then known that he was a son in law of one of the wealthiest people in the valley and himself also a big arts merchant. After I wrote her prescription she got up and turned back to leave, while her husband took out some cash notes to pay me my fees. In the process he dropped a few notes by mistake down on the floor and himself walked away following his wife. Immediately I put my foot on the cash and hid it, drew it with a scratch of my shoe closer to my chair. After a pause, I picked up the money and after counting dropped it in to my table drawer, my heart pounding all the while. It was rupees 156/- or so. A while later somebody came in to ask if I had found any cash on the chair which his Sahib(master) had occupied while I saw his wife. With my negative reply he went away as he had come. I felt victorious. Avenged for the insult a rich illiterate person had hurled on me and my profession and all mine- like educated lower middle class. At the same time, I felt sorry for him for his arrogance and I felt sorry for myself for being jealous of his riches and for my revengefulness.

That is about the robbery that I have alluded to earlier visa-vis my patient and the jury needs to pronounce it's verdict 'Guilty or no'. I say it once again that I feel truly sorry.

This world is very large and how and with how many can one be revengeful and keep grudges. It's reward:156/- rupees!

Chapter VI

HUMAN CONFLICTS

Man by nature is psychologically a dependent being. As a child he/she depended upon parents for support both physical as well as psychic. With time it is the parent substitutes real or imaginary that come to provide that. A long dead mother or father are often invoked by people in distress to help them out; a common finding in patients of painful and serious disorders. Mental mechanisms supporting our belief in God, work on the same lines; substituting a male god for the father and a goddess for the mother. Two most important conflicts in human life also are directly or otherwise related to this very mechanism of mind; viz., possession of the female (conflict over sex) and now the well-known conflict over religion (whose God is true?). Other conflicts about land, gold, money and other possessions are derivatives from our civilization and later developments of human society. In it's earliest stages humans started as hunter-gatherers- a nomadic existence. They had no use for gold or what is now called even the prime land. Robinson Crusoe found no use for his gold coins in the isolation of his island.

Religion has been accepted by many great people as a symptom of a universal disease of mind, a self-perpetuating virus in our mental software. It is a calculated miscalculation based on unproved premise and elaborated over time. It is the source and supply of all superstition and most hatred and killings in the world. It originates from an inborn weakness of mind called dependency needs. Every man, howsoever brave, powerful or emancipated and knowledgeable he may be, feels a need for some kind of support from outside especially in times of difficulty. He may even call for his long dead father or mother to come to his help then. This is an obviously illogical thing to do but it consoles. A father who in his own time of difficulty, like when he was himself dying had invoked and begged for help of his own dead father but was obviously not helped or saved by him. How is that possible, after all for a dead person to come to some one's help? But the dying man had a consolation that his father's noble soul will listen to his cries and come to his help, right up to the moment when he too falls silent. Dead means stone dead. Similar magical powers attributed to anything by us do not do, and in reality have no power to do any material good to any one in any situation else than giving a false feeling and hope of support. This is delusive in the least. And that is how and upon what, is all religion based. Religion is a standing monument to man's inner weakness, unreasonableness and his false pretensions of nobility and high character. Religiosity, piety and the associated rituals and worship etc. are secondary developments in the history of religion, the primary kernel being the much needed belief in a higher omnipotent power who could come to one's help in time of need. But it is the secondary developments aimed at pleasing the high power that are causing the most trouble to man now. A person living on external support to stay satisfied and happy is not truly happy. He goes out on one limb to keep his supporter/benefactor pleased; remains afraid of him ever. And when that support as well as the supporter are phantoms and imaginary the methods devised to keep him in good humor also become grotesque and demeaning. Bathing, washing and cleaning of body was declared impious in Christianity and true godly people would wash at best their fore fingers while eating if at all. Body lice so cultivated were termed 'pearls of piety' and often the skin of neck and forehead was not visible due to it's cover of teeming lice. Was that pious godly man happy and enjoying his life? Self-mortification, fasting, self-flagellation and other bizarre means are employed to please the omnipotent god in order to gain heaven and to escape the ordeal of this mortal life. Our sadhus a good proportion of whom are aimless mental patients, in saffron clothes roaming the dusty streets to live on alms in order to see their god and enjoy in next life? Is their existing life well spent and happy? This is to say the least delusive. And finally to cap it all goes their blind faith with it. And for their faith in 'their' god they go about killing and burning people if they don't accept this mad faith and belief. Is this all conducive to a meaningful life? No, neither for them nor for others. Still some people argue that this falsehood is good and a helpful one and so should be encouraged. We whole heartedly dispute! Should a sensible person live upon and cling to falsehood in order to survive? Is it really ethical? I think it was Voltaire who said that if there were no God we ought to make one ostensibly to provide an imaginary support to men. It is wrong advice from a great man. On the other hand the much maligned Machiavelli has realistically advised people in power to exploit their subjugated people by inducing and encouraging religious beliefs and practices among them. And that is what the religious leaders and the entire priesthood are practicing and thriving upon. They live off the suffering and superstition of masses. It is their trade and profession and they leave no stone unturned to increase their grip on the unsuspecting masses. Excommunications, crusades and jihad and religious dictats (fatwas) are resorted to not as much to please the omnipotent god as to stay relevant and in power, further distorting the basic tenets of their religion. These are convenient and profitable methods of staying in power and enjoying it's fruits too. Dispensations and exemptions issued by popes and advance booking of berths in heaven, falls in the same category of falsehoods and reveal the corruption behind religious deals. In any case these take away the very essence and joy of life from the simple multitude. It is their exploitation. It is this sociological aspect of our life which concerns us here, in the discussion on individual happiness.

A person who frenziedly chants hymns rhythmically to his ecstasy top and a person lost in repetitive counting of god's name and praise on beads, forgetting the reality around him get, scientifically speaking, into a semi-hypnotic trance. It is like a mother sending her baby to sleep by timed rhythmic strokes of her hand in it's back accompanied by some lulling sounds; These devotees do the same thing to their mind. They feel joyful, contented and as having gained power over things by having reached that state/stage of worship. But is joy and charm of life gained through autohypnosis and stringent self-deprivations a desirable goal? These are self-induced pathological states of mind. And such are our objections to prevalent religion and it's protagonists. To sum up then religion appears, for one reason or the other, to be the epitome of man's irrationality, corruption and selfishness. Of the purported seven wonders of this world it is certainly the top first. A paradox, an illogical conclusion, which 'man' bases most of his logical conclusions upon. Newton ultimately fell to dabble in theology, mystical dogmas and occult practices wherein, to my knowledge, group worship of male genitals in full erection was practised. This so, after his meteoric discoveries in science. And if that proverbial genius called Newton could fall that low what of ordinary earthlings, what can they not do to obtain a berth in heaven? Why can't the ordinary rif-raf go about shooting and bombing to get their share of 72 hurs at the earliest? And that was the finale of Newton's brilliant life and intellect. Religion can turn anyone blind; mad it's followers already are albeit in degrees! Oh God, am I again talking atheism? Blasphemy! Forgotten hell fires?

The problems created by present day religions are essentially attributable to lack of self-confidence. And religion has done all the damage to man that it could through draining that confidence out of people's hearts by asking them to rely on God to help you in time of need. Gone are the days when people related tales of heroism of men like Achilles, Hercules, Rostum and sorab and their likes. Gone are the days when mothers used to teach bravery and self-assertion to their children by relating life stories of great men like Rana Partap, Shivaji, Ahaliya Bhai, Robert Bruce and his teacher the spider,and their likes.How many boys of present generation have heard the storyof Nachiketa or

Casabianca as examples of obedience to parents.On the other hand, the focus of parents is on their children's achievement in grabbing big positions and earning money somehow, recommendationsand bribing one's way included. Above all they are taught to seek God's blessings and help for that, right from early days. Instead of inculcating confidence in the children's own capacity and the capacity of their heart and brains, they are primed to rely on outside help and imaginary props. An average boy entering an examination hall instead of having a raised head, inflated chest and opened up shoulders indicative of confidence, enters with head bowed and shoulders shrunken as if already half-defeated, with eyes half closed, internally begging his imaginary benefactor for some miracle. Instead friends, tell them to remember 'AhamBrahmosmi'- 'I am the all-powerful, I shall get what I try for'. Instill courage in them and teach them 'Reap what you sow'. I am not preaching atheism, I hope. I am trying to draw attention to a possible philosophy of life, a way of looking at life. It is no religion either, merely a suggestion to have an open self-reliant mind and heart, while you continue to preserve affiliation to your own respectable religion. A self-confident person is joyful even in the worst of circumstances and that joy in life is my concern at the moment. People stranded in open seas like in ship wrecks try to swim and stay afloat till some rescue reaches them. But, it has been observed that those who loose their confidence and hope early during the ordeal are the ones; age and physical health of groups remaining approximately the same, who drown the earliest. Same with people caught in adverse circumstances like in snowy mountains and deserts. Such is the importance of self-confidence in life. Supernatural help is sought most of all by stock exchange manipulators and moneyed business men and landed farmers. The former ask for miracles and the latter for good seasonal rains and protection from elements. Wage earners are by and large less religious and least superstitious. An open less rigid philosophy and least dependence on others in life can help all to stay happy and manly. Even if there is a God up in the sky why should anyone depend upon him for one's survival and day to day happiness. A self-reliant, self-supporting and confident son can be a source of joy and satisfaction to his parents, so also to that all-embracing father, the God. How does one expect that father to stay happy with a son who remains a baby all his life asking to be hand-held by him at every step that he takes? Is god happy with stupid people who refuse to grow up? Dependence on supernatural powers and miracles leads to attempts at pleasing those powers through unreasonable even magical acts and antics. Why does the all-powerful God not prevent misery, deprivation and sorrow amongst his children/creation by himself? And if we ask for joy in life through curtailment of superstitious beliefs and blind faith and an open mind, is that something bad? Are we not doing godly work? That ought to have been his duty. One of the chief methods of making people religious is by inducing a sense of guilt into them. They, from young days are, as stated earlier, asked to seek forgiveness for their sins. Which sins? That is the question! They are advised to fear god's wrath. Over What? This kills that positivity of life. How can a sinner remain happy? Any pleasurable act is automatically connected to his existing dread of sin in his fear primed mind and the pleasure of the action is replaced by a fear of God's vengeance. Is this right? God who is otherwise described as all-merciful (Al-raheem in Arabic) is pictured as a fearsome demon in the so affected innocent mind. Our submission is that He ought to be accepted as a loving father and his mere mention should invoke a sense of love, peace and forgiveness.

The word 'atheist' is also euphemistically applied to a person who respects no norms, convention or tradition. He is a kind of rebel who insists upon examining things for himself and rejects what is not empirically and scientifically verifiable. The new age religion! Believe in your own self, not in delusions. I am glad that Advaita philosophy of Vedanta approaches this rationalistic thought the nearest by declaring 'AhamBrahmosmi'viz I am God –a slogan nearest to what is called atheism by the pious believers; Every bit of this universe is God including us and must not be harmed. Sufi Islam is another such rational, tolerant and all welcoming religion. It has no place for hatred. Maulana Rumi, one of the greatest ever, was a Sufi poet. Like our Chaitanimahaprabu he sang of love, only-love for all and everything. Concepts like 'AhamBrahmosmi' give self-confidence and some sense of self-respect too.We are not, afterall, puppets in someone else's hands. Perhaps I am an agnostic not an outright atheist-fit neither for grave nor the cremation pyre. Destined for 'eternal damnation'? My God, please save 'my soul'!'.

 But my God is a loveful God not a jealous god. He does not say 'There is no God but Me and I reside up-up in the sky, and keep account of all you do and will punish and reward you at my discretion'. A rationalist's reply to such a god: 'Sir, have you no other work except peeping into other's affairs? Who has appointed you for what you are? Why do you spoil the charm of our lives'? Studying the history of religion, even a little, can be consoling as it relieves the rigidities in our mind; the rigidities introduced by flagrant application of religious tenets and dogmas as and what suits the priesthood and the related bosses. Pleasure of any kind in life is, as a rule, prohibited for the commoners!

Religion of primitive people was animistic and every hamlet and every clan had its own spirits and angels both good as well as bad to propitiate and to seek protection from. It was an easy affair. They had no use for converting any one to their faith because everyone was ready to accept every spirit or ghost for it's value. Even far later in the evolution of society, it would take no blood shedding or wars for Romans to take up to worshipping Greek Gods or the Egyptian pantheon. Julius Caesar peacefully accepted the supremacy of Egyptiangoddess Isis and back in Rome would not hesitate to declare himself a God in the way of Egyptian queen Cleopatra and her fore-runners. Polytheists and nature worshippers who were called 'Pagans' by later Christians were most easy with their faiths and accommodated different belief systems with benign indifference. Greeks and Romans along with all north Europeans like franks, Goths, Nordics etc. were all polytheists and pagans. **Historically, the first monotheistic (one god) religion was founded (Invented) in Egypt by Pharoah Amenhotep iv around 1375 B.C.**Heordered decimation of all statues and temples of the then prevailing Egyptian polytheistic gods. Worship of one universal god 'Aton' was propagated and priests of the old religion were actively persecuted. It must have involved some blood shed too. Hence, we see religious intolerance and violence initiated for the first time in human history in the name of and for the glory of 'One and only one supreme god'. And this 'One supreme God' has never allowed humanity any rest ever since his discovery by the Egyptian pharaoh. His name, designation and forms have changed with every new reformer or prophet coming up but monotheism goes strong as ever through the use of stake or the sword of his faithful followers. Some kill in order to' save the souls 'of men and some in order to send people to heaven to enjoy with 'Hurs and fairies'.

The custom of male circumcision, is proved historically to have originated in Egypt prior to Mosaic era and was later continued in two of three Abrahamic religions giving it a central religious importance. Geographical distance between eastern Egypt and Jerusalem and Mecca is not much and the ideas of 'one and only one supreme god' as also of circumcision, permeated around and were absorbed in Judaism and Islam. Originality of these lies in Egypt historically nonetheless. Similarly the word 'Amen' seeking to confirm a prayer or blessing used by followers of all the three religions derives from the ancient cry/desire of followers of the religion of

'Amon-Ra', ' May Amenhotep the pharaoh'(the God) grant the request/prayer! And so unknowingly the present religious' men are seeking to be blessed by Amenhotep's of Egypt, even today. The word 'Amen' has got incorporated into Hebrew and the meaning attributed now to it is 'So be it' but its roots lie in Egypt. Common usage by three different religions points to a common origin as do their many other commonalities.

Before proceeding any further in my talk of religion I must clear my own position with regard to it by stating that my head and heart are at variance on this controversial subject. After all who has seen God? And who has seen heaven or hell as described by various religions? Yet these inventions of human mind have snatched much peace of humans ever since their discovery in Egypt by the Pharaoh. Shouldn't one's reason and conscience rebel against dogmatic and authoritative declarations made by some religious people on the basis of documents written in old ignorant times. Scientific investigation has so far failed to confirm these claims. On the other hand we know that spiritual experiences as described by various people could just be products of an abnormal or diseased mind. In fact religious delusions and clear visions of God's blessing their believers are not uncommonly met amongst frankly insane individuals. There are mental states of abnormality wherein symptoms are characteristically and typically of religious rituals and chants and these we treat scientifically. Should we disbelieve what our eyes and ears see and hear and instead believe myths and hearsay? In my opinion any declaredly spiritual person who is advertised as a saint can only be either a mental patient or a cheat. In any case, the less said is better. Presently we go back to our historical narrative!

In India, in contrast Mohenjo-Daro and Harappa in the Indus valley had flourished some 2000 years earlier, with all their town planning and village administration etc. Oldest images (Idols) of gods anywhere in the world have been found in these excavations and these are of 'Shiva' called 'Rudra' in the Vedas and also of mother goddesscalled 'Shakhti'.Ramayana and Mahabharata were learnt by rote and transmitted verbally from generation to generation during the so called'Epic' period around 1700 b.c. (before Christ) Sanskritisation of south India and the spread of Shiva and Narayana (Vaishnav) cults headed perhaps by sage Augustia Muni perhaps happened around 1500 b.c. These dates are evidence based and so historical. Tradition places them far earlier in time. Imagine the religious, intellectual and social development of this country vis-à-vis the rest of the world by these facts, and in those times.I don't want to sound jingoistic but the fact is that when the concept of one supreme God 'Brahman' was articulated in the Upanishads, the Mosaic (of Moses) and later so called Abrahmic religions were nowhere near even conception. Buddha and Mahavira in India and Confucius and Lao Tse in China lived around 6 to 7 century B.C. but all had avoided the pitfalls of starting a 'One and only one god' religion and so there never occurred any killings or persecution amongst their followers neither in China nor in India or elsewhere. Hinduism had accepted polytheism and even animism as it's parts and weaved these into it's web alongside it's basic emphasis on one universal God- Brahman or Parameshwar and thus saved it's followers from internecine and even inter-religious conflicts and fighting. Two Hindu philosophical schools viz. Sankhya and Yoga are essentially atheistic in concept and practice. These too form part of the Indian religious juggernaut and exist peacefully along.

I believe, no religion can allow man to be happy as long it's God is portrayed as a master who has the power to punish with hell fires,while man stays in the position of a slave and when all pleasurable activity has been labeled a sin.

MY RELIGION; Earlier I had deferred talking about my own position and thinking about God and religion and now the above description of the subject allows me some leeway. I am born a Hindu and the native

Samaskars and culture has seeped into me and I am so to say 'Dyed in the wool'. Godliness or any firm unquestionable, belief in the existence of God is not an essential part of Hinduism or it's other two sister belief systems of Budhism and Jainas and this has come to me as a great relief in my life. We don't have to provide any definite time/s for worship and so no interference in the pursuit of life occurs; in fact regular repeated obligatory worship times would have impinged upon my sense of independence and as it is I feel free/er. It allows me to show respect to everyone else's god and belief system from a comfortable distance and I am happy for that. In my childhood our friends were a mixed lot, most of them Muslims. But it never entered our heads to count or value each other in terms of religious affiliation nor did we ever hear our parents advising us about our friend's religions. At the women's level interdining was prohibited but men folk and in particular my own father took to it with pleasure. A school friend who later continued with me at the college too despite coming from a devout family has never talked to me or us- his Hindu friends anything about his or our religion but now bemoans the ugly shape our new times have taken. The Quranic injunction 'Lakum din-u-kumwaliya din' (to you your faith and me my faith welcome) has been forgotten.

Now, what you may call a childlike thinking on my part: Like the old Grecians for whom their gods came down from their high abodes to help them, to console them in time of difficulty or destroy an enemy in war etc. etc. and for whom I have a special love in my heart, I tend at times to indulge in a special personal relationship with 'My God'. A personal god who has come to my help many a times like the Greek gods. I believe him to be a friend of mine who listens to me when I remember him and also helps me in time of need. Believe it I talk to him when I need him much and can, surprisingly, hear him talk but only when it is extremely important and my prayer really ardent. I never feel He needs to be propitiated or worshipped in order to make him happy with me. I love my friend and the relationship is reciprocal, I believe.

Imagine how colourful the mental life of those Greeks (hellens) was while they imagined God Zeus, scepter in hand, fly down from his high abode in Olympus in order to help his friend in time of his need; the high goddess Athena in her divine costume and the lesser gods like Venus, mercury, Aphrodite, the sun god Phoebus in his chariot etc. wind and the fire gods mounted on their respective carriers, in their magnificentcolourful dresses fighting for or arguing the case of their protégé amongst themselves or with their human adversaries. Truly a gorgeous pageant; a divine procession in all shapes and colours passes before one's eyes. Add to this their temple of Delphi with it's oracles and one finds that these Hellens had created a universe of their own. I fail to make out how Bachhus (God of alcoholic beverages) looked like and how he blessed his devotees and what with. No wonder, the contribution to art, architecture and literature and verily to life in general that these imaginativeHellens made is outstanding. Perhaps nothing less could be expected from such people who are very ably represented by the names of Socrates, Plato and Homer and a galaxy of such eminent men. It should be remembered that these Hellens were not the original residents of Greece but Aryans of the same stock who descended into India and made this country their home and are called the Indo-Europeans. Their contribution to Indian life has been no less. Our Upanishads the fountain-head of all Indian philosophy and religious thought and the famous epics are the produce of the same fertile minds. Our pantheon of lesser Gods is in no way smaller or less colourful and full of life than what they produced in Greece. Only our Gods are less flamboyant exhibiting a peculiar serenity, in keeping with the contented atmosphere prevailing naturally in this land. But we cannot ignore the harmless intrigues and backbiting of gods done by 'Narada' the court jester and joker for the gods to laugh and relax and enjoy like the Greek gods. Peace (Shanti) has however, like in ancient China been the byword here ever. Ancient art and architecture produced by these Indo-aryans in India was/is of no less in quality than what they contributed in Greece in particular. Only we were unfortunate in having waves of barbaric hordes visiting us from time to time to destroy our heritage in the name of their God and religion. Sword to kill and crowbar to raze and demolish followed by the faithful to convert was their mission.

GREECE AND SPARTA; Even now the qualification of 'Spartan habits and life' applied to someone is a compliment, and speaks of high integrity, cleanliness, immaculate conduct, austere and simple, no-non-sense style of life. Athens gave itself a selfless administrator and statesman in a famous person called 'Pericles' who ruled Athens for 30 years and the heights of prosperity and happiness reached in Athens under him was exemplary. Athens was then called Pericle'sAthen. What heights of excellence they achieved in their short life of 150 years the Romans failed even to copy or even continue, during their sway lasting double that period? The latter employed slave Greek teachers to teach them books and Greek physicians to treat them when sick. The edifice of the much touted Roman Empire rested on the shoulders of slaves and their life's pleasure on their sadistic and cruel torture and exploitation while their food came from an enslaved Egypt and areas around.

Persians in their east with their oriental culture looked down upon Romans as wicked uncouth people greedy for wealth and gold. In fact when Crasuss the third triumvirate (the other two beingJulius Caesar and Pompey) invaded Persia for loot he was captured and molten gold was poured down his throat to make an example for greedy Romans. The Greeks have left burningexamples of heroism and patriotism and civility for others to admire and follow like in the defence at Thermopylae by Spartan Leonidas and his 300 men.The Romans fought with mercenaries and slave soldiers. This is not to berate the Romans entirely but for a comparison. Latin language of the Romans still inspires the development of western languages, English and French in particular. Their cultural hold on the western mind cannot be overestimated. Vergil and Horace were Romans. Modern legal code is based on a Roman prototype called the Justinian law.

About Hindu religion: This religion along with it's twin sisters of Buddhism and Jainism is the only major religion which allows it's followers complete freedom of belief and action(rituals) in combination with intellectual satisfaction if sought by any. It's most valuable contribution to human thought and civilization is the dictum that God is everything and everywhere and so every being is God himself. (The famous Persian poet Hafiz declares "Insankibadbakhtiandaz se baharhai, KambakhatKhuda ho karbandanazarataahai". Meaning: 'man's ill-luck is inestimable; he is himself the God but has turned into a downtrodden wretch.') This concept teaches self-reliance and leaves no scope for the 'God in sky up' to come to anyone's help or for his partisanship in any dispute. 'No chosen people' and so no quarrels. Also no heaven or hell, up in sky; everything here and now, according to one's actions here. Reap as you sow!

According to such thinking, any person who loves India wholeheartedly and respects it's traditions is a Hindu. Religion is not a determining factor, Hinduism being no religion in the sense that other organized religions are. It is a way of life and thought. No compulsions or directions for gaining heaven or reaching God!

Swami Vivekananda thought that a Hindu should believe in Vedas and refrain from eating beef. In any case we must realize the times do not remain the same and our thinking must change with these. Politicians from both sides, more Hindus than Muslims, have attributed a fearsome image and meaning to the word 'Hindu'. It has come to be resented by many to say that all residents of India are Hindus irrespective of their professed religion. The best course under the circumstances should be that

all residents declare their nationality as: HINDUSTANI"
instead. Then word Hindu will come to represent only
those traditionally called so. Alama Iqbal has also
accepted this nomenclature for himself and for all of us.
But the other two conditions must be strictly followed by
all viz: love for the mother land and respect for it's
traditions.

After this detour we must say that adherence to caste
system prevailing still, even though in villages only, is
disgusting. Expected to exist only in the upper castes, it
appears to me a wonder to see it's practice among the
lower and even the lowest of caste groups. While as they
resent being discriminated by their higher caste bearers
they themselves practise it against those who stand lower
in category than their's. One such subcaste won't eat
from the other sub-caste's hands and so on. They don't
invite each other to their family or religious functions
and if invited don't attend. More wondrous for an
outsider; the lower castes as a whole avoid mixing with
or eating from the hands of upper castes, treating them
with equal contempt. It is a tortuous world. Having
visited many such 'Low caste' homes for work or more
for the sake of relieving my heart's ache I found most of
them equally religious, observing all Hindu rites and
rituals in a general manner as well or even more than the
upper castes. Their homes display pictures of same

Hindu gods and Goddesses and in general they appear more religious, pious and cleaner than most so called upper caste people. Some of India's greatest saints have arisen from these lower castes. To name but a few like Tukaram, Kabir, Narayan guru, Matanga and his daughter Matangi and a galaxy of them many of whom taught and guided their Brahmin and other so called upper caste disciples. Then how come they have remained in the lower rungs of society. Previously it must have been due to economic reasons; the poor being set upon by the welloffs, but now it is positively being encouraged and perpetuated for political reasons. Our present day sensation hungry media plays a positive role in extolling caste differences in it's own peculiar manner. If for example someone murders someone else, the presswallas at once dig the caste roots of the parties and if the murdered happened to come from any lower strata it is head lined as 'Dalit murdered' as if murder of any non-dalit would not be worthy news.

Exploitation of the poor and the landless by the rich and the capitalist is no new thing in this world but their political exploitation by them is and the art seems to have been perfected by some politicians here. Must say that I have come to hate and abhor the words 'Upper class' (swaranjati) and the word 'Dalit' among Hindus. Both these words symbolize mischief and in the end the whole religious clan of Hindus stands divided for sake of votes.Lately they have carved out a new religion out of Hindus of Karnataka, with a slogan 'declare that you are not a Hindu and we will give you reservation in everything'. Democracy has come to the help of Hindus and their Hindustan. How I wish Nehru were born sterile or better still impotent. The Mountbatten curse over the land would have been avoided in the latter case.

Caste problem is at base a class conflict, here taking one colour and there a different one. Modern west is riddled with caste of gold, the rich and poor, black and white and so on. Mass shootings in America of white children in schools and of blacks in gatherings are no better than mass killings by Islamists the world over and represent the worst signs of class conflicts in that ideal society that shouts of human rights violations in other lands. Is it the coal calling kettle black? The Romans had Patricians and the plebeians and also slaves free and bonded all separate castes with no less restrictions and hatred of each other. Until very recent times women with no franchise, no right to property formed a separate caste in Europe; they were no better than slaves of past. Muslims with their sunni, shia, wahabi, Ahmadia , Bohra and other sects have added the castes of 'Ashraf (Patricians)' and 'Mussallahs' (plebians who are looked down upon by the former)to their divisions in India. Their 'castes' don't stop at discriminating between each other but they kill each other with impunity in order to go to heaven which abounds in 'Hurs'(fairies). In short humans have never been without a caste. Perhaps the only place where it had been rooted out was the Soviet Union proving the Marxian belief that economics determines man's societal make up, it's belief systems and it's laws. And accordingly land distribution amongst the landless is the way out of this slur of caste. Land must belong to it's tiller.Abolish absentee land -lordism please.

While on the subject of human deprivations and forced degradation, I am reminded of Tennyson's words.

Old order changeth yielding place to new,
Lest one good custom should corrupt the world, And God fulfills himself in many ways.
Much was expected of democracy at it's birth in the triumphant shadows of French revolution and the American declaration of independence and 'WE' also gave ourselves a democratic constitution to follow, nearly three quarters of a century ago. But one is often reminded of the famous speech of Martin Luther King Jr. "I have a dream...." Our constitution also has given our poor and landless Indians, 'a bad check' uncashable at the bank of freedom, liberty and happiness, contrary to what was promised.

Anything, any system or any law needs a change; must change to remain living and useful and so must our constitution as per Tennyson's axiomatic words. It's internal parts are creaking though still working; it's body- it's whole gestalt has become moss laden and rusty. It no more feels for, and provides for the common man at the base of pyramid. It has been usurped by political charlatans and cheats and their super rich cronies.

Most people in India will agree that the 'good custom of democracy' has corrupted this country as well as itself, in it's sway of seven decades. Has it grown senile? No! But too much of anything proves bad and too much of freedom is no exception to this rule; it has been misused. It has poisoned our atmosphere too much. It needs change. Perhaps a short spell of benign dictatorship, like that of Mustafa Kemal Pasha in Turkey Or a spell of presidential form of government with unlimited powers like what was granted to President Roosevelt in America during the great depression. But where to search for another Mustafa Kemal Or Roosevelt in this country? Perhaps the one party government of China could be copied. In the latter case the ruling party having after all been put in power by the majority can continue while the other parties must be legally banned for a limited period of 5 years at the end of which period elections must decide the future rulers and the humdrum and machinations and maneourings of the so called democracy can resume. President's power during the interim can overlook a peaceful transfer of power. These changes must come in constitutionally, and be provided for in a revised document. Perhaps this is too much asked for, but a mature electorate should understand it's needs. Whatever is done must be done peacefully and legally. Legal experts can perhaps suggest some method.

Of what use is a vote manipulated by falsehood, deception and power? Of what use is it to a person whose belly is empty? There are crores of landless people in India while as great landlords owning hundreds of acres of land and going about in luxury cars are designated 'Farmers' with free subsidies of all sorts enjoying tax free incomes and loan write-offs. These are de-facto agricultural industrialists masquerading as farmers. The first job of any people's government must be to treat 'land hunger' and then to wipe out the great cancer of caste in India. But no so- called democratic government can slice off the very branch on which it is perched by declassifying rich land owners and by declassifying the vested interests among the so-called lower castes by simply calling them 'The below poverty line people' granting them more benefits than they get under the abhorrent caste classification. The political party's adept in falsehood and deception will misrepresent these attempts before the illiterate masses and attempt creating chaos in order to gain power for themselves. One single administrator or one single ruling party with a democratic majority but with no fear of political blackmail only can rid our society of these cancers and a five-year term after every 15 years of so-called democratic rambling should prove a panacea for all our afflictions. My pious hopes! They are my private ruminations and can be laughed away. Too simplistic and dreamy!

In dis-affected times who doesn't wish for a change? And so these futile daydreams. But who thought of giving **democracy** and it's accompanying vote to a billion plus illiterate people? In fact, all the ills that are attributable to democracy may not be the fault of this system. It is a common finding that when a Govt. claims, for example, to have built so many roads in the country, most of the populace individually puts back a retort: but what have I got out of that? The same with other forms of general development, "Areymujeiss se kyamila"? And lo, they get leaders they deserve, and they give them laptops, TVs and the like and for themselves swindle thousands of crores from the exchequer. Democratic deal! American president Obama did India a great honour internationally, by being our chief guest on our republic day. But what did he give? Was the common question. No laptops!

Unfortunate as the state of our mobocracy is, please permit me to remember and reminisce some **happier moments of my childhood** and earlier days for a change and this may amuse you too. The older amongst us may remember that about a half century or more ago there was a concept of 'enjoying a ride' say on a bicycle or a horse driven carriage called 'Tonga' etc. We as children enjoyed it much to stealthily get on the foot boards of a tonga and so to be carried some distance till the tonga driver would detect from the carriage's tilt towards the back that some 4 or 5 children had clung to his back. And then would follow a swift but light lash of his wip towards us forcing us to jump down. The experience was exhilarating. We also revealed if some known cyclist would give us a lift seated on the front pipe of his cycle, no matter that we had to traverse that distance back on foot. But the journey was full of happiness and laughterbesides that uplifting sense of achievement. Till not very distant days I had thought that this behavior of our's was primitive and shameful but it came as a relief when I read Charles Dickens reporting that as children they too enjoyed these 'Rides' in London as we did here. Children are alike where ever you go, only men find themselves different; some high and some low, some great and others small etc. etc.

Another example of my 'primitiveness' may also amuse. I as an inhabitant of Kashmir had never seen a train till I arrived in Calcutta by air for my medical studies. Enroute my air travel I had to stop at Delhi where I was stupefied by finding young boys and girls in a restaurant in Connaught place drinking some liquid from hand held bottles which it did not take me long to conclude being alcohol bottles. I ran away from the restaurant to complete my eating seated on a bench in the central park of the area. A Cold drink bottle had horrified me.

Reaching my hostel in Calcutta, I spent one full day at the Sealdah railways station watching railway engines and their attached bogies move on iron rails. My wonder knew no bounds at seeing this marvel puffing out steam below and smoke above.It's giant levers moving/pushing the engine's big wheels looked to me the ultimate expression of man's power to harness nature's force. For my own benefit I made a forecast that man's greed for more and more of everything will one day give us the power to move at blinding speeds in or with the help of rockets. The weight of those rockets to be so used for mass travel worried me however and I divined that steam power generated with the help of sun's heat concentrated with powerful lenses fitted in the body of the rocket, should be able to propel those giant rockets carrying hundreds of people in their belly, just like my dream steam engine did while it roared, whistled and sped away holding it's chimney aloft in majestic vanity. Back at the hostel, the story of my discovery of the steam engine created fun and laughter among the students and many called me a 'Junglee' having come down a barbarian from the mountains of my home land in Kashmir. But I felt triumphant!

Children and ordinary simple minded people don't need to search for pleasures and happiness in life.It is just by their side every moment.But when they grow up they are deconditioned gradually according to the rules of society.While as a 50 rupee note makes a young boy hilarious and jubilant,the same boy later after he has become a big mill magnate doesn't even feel a smile by a gain of 5 lac rupees That boy's needs were limited and he was happy,the mill magnate's needs are unreasonably great and nothing makes him happy. Why can't weinstead of quarreling over whose god is true and whose false just devote ourselves to being happy in whichever position we are in?

My youthful phantasy also ran wild when I thought of a motor-car that could run on mechanical thrust of huge special alloy coiled springs forcibly compressed to release their potential energy in controlled conditions to power a car engine. Cost of fuel in cars bothered me much even though I did not own one. India's dependence on imported oil irked me much. Oh, myfanciful daydreams!

A COINCIDENCE REMEMBERED;in the same vein I relate an unusual happening, nothing great about it perhaps; a mere coincidence the likes of which happening are often related by people and soon forgotten. But I have remembered it this long because similar co-incidences of meaningful nature have occurred to me many times in my life. Add to it my childlike mentality of pagan beliefs and the picture of my superstitious self or my non-superstitious self, as you may like to call it, is before you. There was a great analytic psychologist Carl Jung who was considered by some to be the one of the most knowledgeable men alive at his time. He developed a theory "Synchronicity" to explain similar coincidences as part of what is called Extra sensory perception. He was in contact with Einstein too who encouraged him to consider such happenings in the light of Quantum theory perhaps himself impressed by Jung's thought. If a particle (a quantum of energy) can exist at two places at the same time mysteries in our world seem to get solved by themselves. Another physicist Pauli known for 'Pauli Effect' and close to Einstein, too believed himself, like me, to be a medium for such mystical experiences/happenings. Oneness of underlying cosmic consciousness is considered to cause 'Acausal connection' to effects somehow. Freudian analytic school does not recognize Jung's Universal unconscious nor his Archetypes though they accept a phyletic (borne over previous generations) unconscious. In any case there is no scientific verification for such claims.

Some dreams are known to display prophetic value with many people but only some of them. Most are the garden variety mostly concerned with wish fulfillment as shown by Sigmund Freud.

Long ago I had applied for admission to M.S. in surgery at Delhi University and was awaiting a positive response from there in view of the fact that I had what was believed then to be a good %age of marks in the subject. As the days passed by my tension and expectation grew exponentially and gradually dejection overtook me. One morning I took stock of the days that had elapsed from the last date of application and was filled with gloom. By noon my anger at having trusted my God too much over- took me and in a fit got up and tore to pieces the two photographs of 'Shiva' that were hanging in my room. Not stopping there, I threw those pieces of paper out into our brick lined compound and then rushed to trample upon those with my shoes. My wife all the time stood immobile puzzled by my abrupt madness but I wouldn't care. Every step I took to mangle and massacre the bits of paper, appeared giving a lot of relief in my heart, while suddenly I heard a knocking at the door. To answer this, I collected myself and brushed my disordered hair with both hands and ran to open the door. Lo! What I see is the local postman delivering a telegram. Quickly read, it said "Admitted M.S. Surgery under Dr. K.C. Mahajan Wellington Hospital deposit 109/- rupees fees within 2 days." I read the telegram over and over again and now did not know how to repair the damage I had done by blaspheming my god; my true friend. I hurriedly collected the paper pieces to paste them together and with an apologetic heart hung the crumpled, torn pictures back at their places.

RELIGION AND CRIME; According to Christian mythology the first murder that man committed was by the elder brother Caine of his younger brother Abel. Though the scriptures are silent about it's because it is often believed that Adam and Eve - the first in human creation of God, had many children, both girls and boys. So the brothers quarreled over possession of one of their sisters whom each wanted to marry. Incest has a very long history among humans and was socially accepted amongst Egyptian pharaohs. Even Cleopatra was supposed to get married to her brother but history had a different role for her and a story to play out with Roman monarchs. Freud hints at continuation of incestual marriages amongst European monarchy of yore. So incest between close relations like father- daughter, brother-sister etc. that is so shocking to us now may not be so scarce as the common man believes. Rape however is the commoner variety of human sexual drama. More about that in pages to come.

In Urdu there is a word called 'Fitna' meaning the root or cause of a dispute or feud. And woman has often been termed 'the colourfulfitna '(RangeenFitna). God's position accordingly grows to a 'colour-less or shapeless fitna'. Based on the childhood position of omnipotence in the life of a child and the total erasability of their unconscious memory God's existence and omnipotence has become undeniable despite scientific claims and proofs to the contrary. Even the most rational and scientific people, while accepting the findings of science about life, it's evolution, factual evidence about the start of universe and it's working as per laws of physics, feel unconsciously compelled to believe in God and then to fight and kill in his name and for the greatness of 'their' god. More blood has been spilled and misery heaped upon men in the name of god and religion in world than was spilled in world wars. One of the greatest prophets – Moses, was according to research of the literature on the subject, killed by his own followers, in the same game of religion.

As already stated my head and heart happen to be at variance on the issue of religion and God. Many great people and thinkers have declared that there is no God and the general belief in god is but a general illusion, a mirage. Since this mirage is universal it is accepted as a normal and correct one, any deviation castigated and non-believers looked down upon. Despite the fact that no one has seen heaven, young Jehadis are lately being enticed by promises of 72 'Hurs' (fairies) each in heaven and also a 100 times of their sexual prowess to cope with those ' hurs'.But who and how did those issuing these edicts come to know this tantalizing news from the other world . Yet the fanatics who are trained from childhood onwards to have blind faith in all things religious, believe in this nonsense and die for the 'Hurs'. Ironically, what is promised in their heaven to female Jehadis and suicide bombers has not been told? -72 wrestlers each along with 100 times more strength to withstand the grind! How do people believe this? Human gullibility can be immense and in matters religious, is reinforced by repetitive incantations of the same message in a group dressed and uniformed in similar manner, military style and stressing austerity in life, a white kurta and pajamas with a white Fez (topi) on top.

These messages are almost indelibly stamped into the young impressionable mind. Group discipline and collective belief so developed help it self-feed itself. Combined with regular repeated exhortation from their trainers and teachers it reaches the effects of hypnotism and auto-suggestion. Absolute impermeability of this belief system so created is a proof of it's hypnotic and trans fixated roots. It is in the interest of all countries and in particular this land of secular Gandhi and Nehru that religion must not be allowed to be taught to children below 18 years outside their homes. Group teaching of religion in schools and religious premises needs to be banned if more jehadis and jan-nisaries are to be stopped in formation. In the name of democratic liberty no one can be allowed to breed serpents to be let loose in other's compounds.

There is nothing new in recruitment of young children for purposes of Jehad. In Ottoman Turky they would snatch young Christian boys from their parents in Caucasus and then train them in military art while they grew up as fanatical suicidal fighters for their new religion. They were called 'Jan-nisaries' viz ready to sacrifice themselves. In Egypt similarly young children used to be indoctrinated to sacrifice themselves on call for religious purpose, they were called 'mamelukes' It is amusing to know that when Napoleon invaded Egypt one mameluke captain came forward to challenge the Italian forces for a singular combat. He was met by a burst of gunfire. This backwardness of outlook with an attempt to wind the universal clock backwards has been the bane of such forces. A religion that cannot adjust itself with the scientific forward-looking world but wants to recreate the conditions of 7th century or earlier and be governed by the laws prevailing then, is naturally creating friction and what was called by Huntington as the clash of civilizations. But clashes can occur spontaneously, without any preplanning and when intelligent planning and preparations on a big scale enter the field it becomes a war-now a war of cultures. Having realized the practical invincibility of the Christian world and their combined might in particular of America and it's president Trump, the Jehadis have planned to cunningly infiltrate the European citadels till a critical population ratio is achieved to declare their aims openly. And since that population already exists in strength in India and the place stands encircled on three sides naturally the Jehadist flags are already getting unfurled on proper occasions in proper places. 'Four wives here and seventy-two hurs later' Allah is great!

Christianity has in contrast adjusted itself with the new world order though reluctantly and no more for example insists that universe was created by God 6000 years ago.

It's silence even of a doubtful kind, in matters scientific is a great step forward from burning people at stake for heresy. It would prefer people forgetting it's past but pursues it's policy of proselytizing the ignorant and the helpless poor relentlessly. Why can't people live and let live peacefully!

A racial collective unconscious developed over millennia and gathering strength with every new generation also contributes and makes reception of newly prescribed religious knowledge easier. A lighter term for this past learning transmitted unconsciously to the newer breed could be our Hindustani word of 'Samaskars'. Human or more correctly racial or national or group, culture and civilization derives largely out of these samaskars. As stated we do get mental patients who declare having seen god and talked to him. Such a declaration by them is usually accompanied by accepted signs of frank insanity and one can make out that those declarations are part of their disease. 'It is the very coinage of their brain'. Apart from this it is perhaps not possible to find a man who can sensibly and verifiably prove such an occurrence without having a motive for so doing, as is seen in the teachers of young jehadis. In past, dark ignorance, belief in superstition and absence of communication made people to   believe and accept deluded mental patients who declared to be in communion with God as saints and spiritually great. The origin of many cults and some religions is traceable to similar happenings when miracles and prophesies were attributed to those so called spiritual men. As everyone knows there is also no dearth of such ingenious god-men even in 21st century and many of these carry a sizeable following. But as modernity takes hold even in Asian and African hinterland such people are sent for psychiatric treatment or the police takes care of them. Epilepsy, in ancient Europe and the Semitic world was considered a sacred illness and perhaps Julius Caesar also suffered from it. I personally do not believe in miracles- events and things that can happen and not be explainable scientifically. Even one such miraculous happening would be a great support to a person ridden with doubt. But alas, I know of none. Adding to my doubts, I as a psychiatrist have seen religiosity rampant among mental patients of all grades; the less severely ill patients of neuroses appear otherwise quite normal for their day to day activity. In fact the more neurotic a person the worse his religiosity could be and his belief in god may be a central peg that he holds as a support in his precariously balanced world. The more insecure he is internally the more rigid his belief system. More about this later!

Chapter VII

A MIXED BAG

First a PERSONAL EXPERIENCE (mother India) I have interrupted the last chapter suddenly to talk of a pleasurable experience which came my way today forenoon. This liberty I am taking because I am, like most writers and especially artists drawing much from my own life; so other things can await our leisure.

I am in the habit of taking a short break during my clinic hours; usually after I have seen a few patients, I ask my remaining patient's permission to go out for a few minutes. This is for a quick smoke "(WARNING: Smoking causes cancer)". Unmindful of this "statutory warning", this morning I took my seat on a parked scooter in the street downstairs and lighted up. Suddenly my eyes fell on a group of students from the neighbouring college, standing in front of the cigarette selling shop. They were 2 boys and a girl, happy and hilarious looking. They were also smoking, engrossed in themselves, quite informal- innocent friendship. Somehow I took note of the girl in particular and it pleased me to see her holding a cigarette in her hand as she blew out smoke in gusts watching it go up and vanish. I felt she enjoyed it more than I personally had at many occasions in past done. She savoured it and felt at ease and relaxed. A heavy weight was as if lifted off her as the same blew up in smoke and vanished. The atmosphere in the group was jovial and chirping mixed with smiles and smooth gestures continued unmindful of what was happening around. They were perhaps talking unmeaning gossip but enjoying the moments every bit. A small world of their own! The girl perhaps talked the least but appeared the centre of the show; once a while smiling but in control. Smoke every puff, thick and white rising up, perhaps signaling some relief somewhere, perhaps deep in the very recesses of heart. Suddenly I realised that I saw thick puffs of white smoke, once or twice taking the shape of a clenched fist as that moved upward to disappear in the lazy polluted air that surrounded us. I felt aghast while the students unmindful of surroundings remained busy in their own chirping and smiles. Innocence of their age when every moment can be sweet and beautiful. Breath-taking! The boys inhaled deep and relished every pull on their cigarettes but the girl threw out the gusts quickly from her mouth like any novice in thick bursts. The cloud appeared far too big for her little puff and I imagined it was bloated by vapours- from her lungs; could be from deep inside her, emanations of something boiling sizzling; steam –pent up steam seeking an outlet, an opportunity to vent out. Was I hearing a muffled voice too along with the raised fists in the outpourings of her breath. Yes, yes, I made sure it was a whisper perhaps sounding **'La Inde', French for Mother India. Joan of Arc had raised 'La Patrie'** (My Father Land) slogan and was I listening to her voice again? I doubted. Yes, perhaps; my little girl was no less. She had also raised the banner against repression, against slavery which she and millions of her ilk and gender were suffering since ages and was shouting 'Mother Inde' like her predecessor. Was it a flag of liberty – of freedom. Yes, she looked free to do anything that pleased her and above all signaled an equality with the boys by not opposing them or criticizing their ways but by gently sharing activities as equals. Not an iota of antagonism or jealousy! A seamless merger!

Women in India have risen to the call of times and this auger well for all of us. A bit of caution here is necessary however. Quarrels between educated working couples are getting frequent and many a times or mostly on money matters. Marriages are planned like business ventures with an eye on the wife's earning to support the planned family and disappointment on this front causes friction. Traditionally, a Hindu marriage is not a contract nor a partnership concern. It used to be the husband's responsibility to meet the household expense and if that be kept in view while welcoming the wife's earning as a source of security and to meet some major expense as these come up, the frictions of a for-profit-enterprise can be avoided. The incidence of male jealousy aroused in cases where wife's income exceeds the man's will also be reduced through a healthy attitude of love, companionship and help and not of competition. Please remember that your wife is not a perfect human being nor are your sir. Deficiency and irregular edges are bound to exist on both sides and marriage involves a compromise and acceptance of each other in an as-you – are state. Adjustments evolve in time. A tale of adjustment follows:

It was in early1960s while in the medical college I met our college Principal in order to get accommodation in the college hostel. He was an elderly man named Dr. Bagchi, bearing the title of Rai Bahadur granted obviously by the English. He accepted to grant me a place in the hostel despite it's fullness on the condition that I should not complain about use of mustard oil in cooking at the hostel mess, having mistaken me for a Punjabi who don't relish mustard oil.I kept quiet not letting him know that I was a Kashmiri and that we too use mustard oil for all cooking like Bengalis do. He quickly fell into a reverie and muttered to me" look boy, adjustment is the substance of and the means to a peaceful life." Going further said "when I was married I found that my wife was using coconut oil in her extra-long hair. Well I hated the smell of coconut oil from an early age and couldn't stand it. But despite my innumerable requests she did not heed changing her oil.

And now after this long a time of our union I find it difficult to sleep without the smell of coconut oil in my bedroom." I as a young boy felt amused and smiled, perhaps at the oddity of life. But now, I agree!

We must talk also about the new wave of consciousness that has arisen among the Muslim women in India lately. They have well agitated against the tyranny of triple Talaaq that has overwhelmed them since ages. And fortunately the law has also come to their help in this matter. I am reminded of a real story of it now which throws light on the inhuman practice of Halala as well.

THREE TALAQ FOLLOWED BY HALALA, an eye witness account: It was in the mid-60s last that We were building our house in Srinagar, Kashmir. One carpenter one mason and three labourers were working at the construction site; all Muslims. Our daily contact made us to get very friendly with each other. As was usual with KashmiriMuslims they showed an extra degree of love and respect for me as an educated Kashmiripandit. So one day the carpenter- a young man in 30s declared that he would arrange for the afternoon tea for the entire party for the next day, since he lived in close neighbourhood of the place. Every one welcomed it. The next day by around 4 o'clock his wife, a pretty smiling young lady in bright coloured clothes brought a 'Samawar' of Kashmiri salt tea to us and herself poured the tea into 6 cups for us to take. It was to the accompaniment of the traditional Kashmiri bread the chhoch-waru. But no sooner did we raise our cups to lips than her young husband threw his cup and the bread down shouting hoarsely on her that the tea lacks salt and that she had thrown his honour and all life's "respect into dust and dirt". Every one tried to calm him by saying that this has been an ordinary and common lapse and that we will ask for some salt powder right then and correct the fault. But of no avail. The gentleman went on cursing the wife declaring her as an incorrigible offender out to spoil him and having planned to make him 'zalil'(wretched) in the world. The woman was weeping shedding inconsolable tears but silent. Suddenly the carpenter in a fit of rage got up to declare that he had thought of divorcing her often in the past but today she had failed in her final test. He continued shouting at her at the top of his voice and suddenly declared in the name of almighty Allah that she stands divorced immediately and shouted the word Talaq, TalaqTalaq thrice at her, his index finger and hand forcefully slashing the air. Every one stood dumb and paralysed and he himself immediately thereafter turned pale, slumping to the ground. We realized he was in acute repentance and horrified by the consequences that dawned upon him after his error. His brother workers asked him as to what a horrific deed he had done and he started crying loudly

–I am undone, I am destroyed. The wife had stopped weeping and looking amazed, stared eyes wide open, on him. Those were agonizing moments for all and his co-workers went into a huddle discussing remedies for what had happened. I was later told that the matter had become a serious one because the man had uttered the oath in the presence of so many strangers and so needed proper resolution as per religious prescripts. This perhaps meant that if no outsider had witnessed the issue it would simply be forgotten between the wife and her husband. Anyway, the by standing workers went into a huddle to discuss the matter asking the carpenter also to join them. After about a half hour a consensus was arrived at, that the lady needs to be married to someone else in order to become eligible to marry the carpenter again. (this is Halala, I was told) The choice of the new husband posed difficulty for the carpenter however. It had been mutually agreed by the five that the mason would take the lady as his second wife for a few days and then divorce her as per plan. The lady all through sat motionless on the ground, perplexed staring vacantly at the air while her fate was being decided. Her eyes dropping a tear or two on to the grass beneath, now and then. Soul weeping tears of agony! Abject helplessness, hopelessness before Divine law. Allah, the merciful Allah living far away, up in the sky, would not naturally listen; no appeal! But he being a male himself perhaps, is merciful to males only? She must break; her heart must split; that is final. Nothing new for women!

Every one of the advisors and decision makers were bemused when the carpenter hesitatingly said that the mason was a young and healthy muscular person with pink cheeks and that he would not allow his wife's over usage by such a strong and healthy man. And then added his suspicion that he might as well not divorce her at all. Finally, the choice fell upon the eldest and a weak looking one among the labourers, a man in his early fifties with an out pouring of grey hair from under his Topi. He agreed to divorce the lady after two or three days and this assurance soothed the mason. Next day it appears that the decision was carried out with proper help from a mullah. It was humorously related that the new bride groom sent a casual message to his existing wife of his inability to come home for some time because he had got 'Trapped into a Nikah'(marriage). More humor followed when it became known the aged man didn't divorce the lady for more than two months. All this while he stayed as a guest at the first husband's house with free food (dainties as per his order) and bed (Daily new bed sheets etc.) provided under guarantee or else the old man would not leave his lady for him no matter how much he begged and kneeled before him. As a rule, he would answer his dolorous petitions for mercy in short and brief 'I am considering everything, don't worry. Am I doing anything against our "Deen" (religion)?' **(Teen talaaq has been banned in India through an act of parliament during the period the book was awaiting publication)**

SELF CONFIDENCE, GIRLS LIKE IT IN MEN; As I relate this tragic-comic tale, and before I go back to where I left my three young collegiate friends I must say that 'Hope' is a wonderful thing. Human life is sustained on hope only. But there is a greater thing available and that is 'Trust' No living being wishes bad for himself; no one likes pain or tensions for himself. Every one hopes for joy and pleasure in life. Girls before marriage keep dreaming of owning a pleasant, happy home with their husbands and beautiful children playing joyously in the forecourt of that dream house etc. etc. A boy in comparison hopes and dreams of a high job and position in life. Hence your new bride comes to you with pleasant dreams of a happy home to you. Give her the chance and freedom to materialize her dreams. TRUST her. Trust is a great wealth in life. The whole world runs on trust. If I lend you a 100 rupees to be returned after 15 days I am unconsciously trusting my own self to be alive after15 days, you to be alive after 15 days, the whole world to be functioning for that period and then your conscience culture, goodness and our existing relationship all at the same time. In short, I have the confidence in myself about all the above and also if anything goes wrong. This self-confidence is needed to manage any affair or relationship in life. Girls also love confident men. They appear promiseful to them and that is what they admire.

I failed once in my final M.D. and a lady friend- a university lecturer in psychology expressed amazement saying that I never appeared to her a person likely to fail. She looked visibly disappointed. It was so because I appeared confident to her and I knew that she had a special corner of kindness for me. Obviously she must have been observing me without my knowing that. The fact of the matter was that my own carelessness had killed me. I had not cared to look at the exam date sheet and programme and messed it up, losing 6 months in the process. In any case let us note how subtly and imperceptibly women judge men. Sexual selection by females is usually not a turbulent process like in the males. It is said that women love with their ears and men with their tongue. More when we come to the subject.

If someone trusts you for anything this is a compliment that gladdens your heart and in return you will try your best to hold that position of trust in his eyes. You will also love him for his trustful manner. If you can trust that your new bride 'will love' to serve you your breakfast as soon as you need that on getting up in morning with her henna painted hands and wearing arm length bright coloured bangles or attend to you during a severe bout of fever etc. you will realize what bliss it confers on you and vice versa. If she is also a working person and has to leave home earlier than you have to and if she keeps your breakfast ready on your bed-side table and your packed lunch ready adding one or two pieces of sweets too, for you to leave before she leaves for her job without disturbing your sleep you should realize how happiness has creeped into your life without you ever having noticed it. That is the bliss of marriage not the money she brings you at the month end. Conjugal love and union reinforces and helps maintain it at it's high pitch till you become more friends in life than mere spouses. It cements the two halves of life into a complete full. I have observed that my wife would prepare the vegetable of my choice for our dinner without my knowledge as if my desire was conveyed to her telepathically. This would gladden me much in the evenings. Perhaps this could be interpreted differently also that since I was very fond of her so whatever she cooked I would sense that dish of my choice was conveyed to her heart somehow in advance. In contrast I have seen couples who share equally the monthly rent of their hired flat and other home expenses including their children's school fees. What joy and satisfaction can one expect from such a commercial pact? If you want a marriage to succeed, then throw capitalism out through the window. It is an inhuman philosophy both inside as well as outside your home. It has killed humanity among humans! The maxim 'From one according to his ability to one according to his needs and satisfaction' was thetraditional family formula. Husband contributed money the wife contributed her manifold services to run the house. Decide whether you want happiness or money from your wife far ahead of your marriage! A woman under ideal middle class Indian circumstances was not supposed to labour for money or to support the home. That is a man's duty. Give your wife her choice of work; if she wants to earn or not. But every girl must be qualified enough to be able to stand on her own legs in case of need in later life. Men these days have become over-Americanised and hence unnatural and untrustworthy in marriage. They have, it seems, lost sight of the very purpose of life in general and marriage in particular.

It is in women's nature to take pride in their husband's position and earning. Most of them would like a husband who is superior to them in practically everything and they spend money with a sense of pride if it is the husband's earning; they like it more than their own earning; I mean they cherish and care for it more than if it was their own earning. In comparison, an average male considers it undignified to live on wife's earning and it is in his nature to feel jealous of the wife who earns more than he does. These traits have developed in the two genders from those early times when we were hunter-gatherers; the male used to go hunting, while the female managed their cave and looked after her children etc.

Relations of your wife visa-vis your parents need to be watched carefully. Parents in law of a lady have their own psychological compulsions. It is the job of a husband as a man to secure his new wife from unreasonable encroachment from his parent's side as much as to secure them from an unruly wife, which phenomenon is mostly a rarity.

Women are often disturbed when critical remarks against their parents or family are made by the husband or his parents. Sensible people usually avoid such things and thus help their own selves. A good maxim for a good marriage is 'Don't berate wife's parents'.

EXAMPLE (Insecure men) A young man working in a multinational company who had come for counseling to me informed that he feared that his wife who has an independent income could leave him any time she finds a better person around. He also related that in case of his premature death the lady will remarry and so take along all immovable assets that be in her name to her next husband.

His first fear was based on half-truths; <u>themselves originating from lack of confidence in particular relating to his sex.</u> Women as a genre do not have the same sexual compulsions as men have. I asked him whether he had ever seen a cow pursuing an ox for mating. No, it is every time the other way round; and this is natural. Women are not men, they are females and their needs, thinking likings etc. are separate and different most of the time. Married women are often heard complaining(laughing) to their husbands that 'you are only after THIS' and you seek me only because of THAT AND NOT FOR MY LOVE. Not that they don't want sex but their need is not as great and urgent as in males. Every woman wants a fit man and feels proud of his fitness but doesn't need his fitness practiced too often. A non-confident man remains ridden with doubts whether he can 'satisfy' his wife sexually and that abnormal desire to somehow impress her compels him to try overdo things. This anxiety to overdo kills his otherwise normal performance, further adding to his tension and confirming his opinion about his inferiority. This in return actually lowers his performance more and more and may render him impotent also. A satisfying and happy mating is essentially a psychological affair and the physical activity involved in it is a natural interaction between two living and feeling creatures. Love and love making are delicate work, don't confuse it with wrestling. If it were otherwise, most women would choose only wrestlers and pehelwans for husbands. The fact is that those wrestlers also are at times divorced by their women, if they don't behave well.

Adultery is not uncommon but in Indian context it is rare and then also the man takes the initiative and the woman may succumb more to please her paramour than for her own sexual enjoyment. As said women's world is not a man's world. It is very different and so are her sexual preferences. Indian women in particular and women in general all over the world value Security in marriage as their most important asset. Even in job matters a woman prefers stability even at the cost of stagnating at the same level than taking risks of changing jobs for promotions. Indian ones seldom will take risks with regard to their marriage. Very highly placed women report so. It is a cultural effect mixed in their blood. This has been dinned into them from their very birth onwards. Tradition can't be underestimated. In case of Americans, they have yet to evolve a tradition and they are doing that now and in that, promiscuity is encouraged in the name of liberty. Here women are horrified by the word 'Divorce' because it has a stigma attached to it in Indian circumstances. A divorced lady has less chance of getting the right man for her husband than a young widow. Premarital sex is a different thing for everyone.

In cases of extramarital relations women somehow bear the misdeeds of their men more commonly though with tears in their eyes than do men bear their wife's infidelity. Further, a woman has the interests of her children close to her heart; even when in the arms of her lover she worries about the social and other affects her aberrant action might have on the future of her children. A woman is born to nurture her breed and it is part of her sexual life to do so. She feels incomplete and hollow if she bears no children. Occasionally they may show more love for the children than for the husband. Men are different. They are by nature suspicious as well as jealous of their women's erratic activities and so intolerant. Remember how Hillary Clinton shielded her husband in case of his famous love affair and oval office dalliance. I am sure Mr. Clinton would have acted differently in case the wife was found betraying him.

The second question raised by my patient about his premature death shows his own insecurity and neurosis because that could occur the other way round also. In any case the children for whom the assets are ultimately meant will not be any loosers, the mother will take care of their interests.

SMOKING,POLLUTIONnow coming back to our tale of my young collegiate friends I am glad to say that it didn't take me much to join them introducing myself as a fellow smoker, a diehard one and then a doctor also. All three welcomed my participation and expressed surprise at a doctor who revels in smoking when an opposite attitude would be more expected. Well, I explained myself truthfully by revealing my smoking history dating 50 years plus to say that I started it at 20 years of age when I too was one like them. Pat came the query about any harm that such long use of cigarettes had caused me which I replied in negative adding that a brother of mine 4 to 5 years younger to me and a total nonsmoker died of lung cancer a few years ago. Well, I could be a fool and perhaps am one, to expose myself to such grievous risk on the basis of false consolations and hope that I will escape harm. But then who escapes death; it comes when it comes. I informed them that I do Yoga regularly stressing on breathing exercises in particular and that perhaps may have saved me from any serious side effects of smoking sofar. I informed them that my smoking started as an unthought of expedition in childish pleasure after seeing my senior roommate in the medical college hostel, lying down on his bed smoking very pleasurably after every food intake. I copied him despite warnings from some friends of getting addicted to it. I was brimming with self-confidence then and so would declare that nothing can make me dependant and continued cigarettes. In final year of medicine, I was married; had a brief introduction to my wife then a bewitching and beautiful lass of seventeen or eighteen. An innocent garden lily! And I didn't know how to receive her and accommodate her in my life or vice versa. As I look back I find that I had merged into her without my knowing that. But alas, I had to leave her soon to go back to college in Calcutta. It proved a very traumatic separation to me and I would spend hours thinking of her and many more hours to wait for the postman to bring her occasional letter, in response to which I would shoot several every day, an action the family naturally resented and she too felt embarrassed by. In the process my studies got neglected and smoking came in handy to pass my time and relieve my tensions. Looking back, I have full realization of how desperate separated lovers feel, the intense pangs of dejection have left an indelible mark on my own heart. This tale came stealthily to my mind while we were talking but I advised them summarily against smoking. In response one of the two boys in the group told us what he thought on the subject of harms of smoking emphasizing that smoking was less harmful than the prevailing air pollution in Delhi. In villages one finds elderly people smoking Hookas in groups hours on end but seldom are serious diseases due to that reported. He concluded that inhaling dusty polluted air round the clock in Delhi was worse than inhaling pure cigarette smoke for a small time in comparison. I did agree. Now an interesting comparison:

"Alcohol kills one person every 10 seconds"-WHO Report for 2012. Add to this the millions of families of alcoholics that are shattered and their children who in their turn become drunkards, mental patients and criminals and one perceives the whole truth. Yet our Govt. sells and distributes this largesse freely in Gandhi's land.

Despite my regularity about yoga and walking, I too had started getting a sense of suffocation in Delhi worse during winter months and I made a plan of going out of the city to a hill station every alternate month the whole summer. It would recompense my breathing system much. This year I took to wearing a facial mask right from Nov. and my sense of suffocation that came on me in Delhi roads has vanished while my smoking continues unabated. I must also say that I perceive a definite difference in the quality of inhaled air with the mask on and then without it. In the latter case I find it irritating to my smoke hardened nostrils as well. In consequence, I have stapled two masks one over the other as my safety shield here, and it is truly beneficial. Perhaps smoking in Delhi is doubly injurious- a combination of suspended particulate matter and smoke but the blame is heaped on smoke only.

PSYCHOLOGICAL HEART ATTACK AND PANIC STATES; are a cause of more tension and worry amongst far more people, mostly young adults, than are real and fatal heart attacks, these psychological problems, drain out all happiness from youthful bodies, most of them males and fill them with gloom and despondency because we have been primed to think of heart diseases as the foremost cause of death especially in young people. It is dinned into the population day in and day out by it'sbeneficiaries and by the media with the result that a general neurosis and anxiety has been created in the public at large. And that is why this topic is included here,

The prevailing situation is such that every kind of pain or abnormal sensation in chest is taken for a heart attack forgetting that heart is not the only organ lodged in our chest. Most chest pains and discomforting sensations arise from muscles and bony structures in and around the chest including the shoulder girdles and the neck. These are magnified and then sustained by psychic causes that have their origin somewhere else in the unconscious mind of the indiums; Doctor's role in perpetuating these unhappy states cannot be underestimated. (Iatrogenic causation. Innate strength and resistance to failure of this organ is forgotten even by the specialists. It is forgotten that this is the only pump (it pumps blood sending that to other body parts) in the world that has been designed and manufactured to work for 50,60, or even for a 100 years and more, without needing any rest or repair. Malfunction or disease of this pump in early age is rare. While awareness about the ill-effects of smoking and drinking etc. is a good thing but incorrect knowledge and disinformation about anything is certainly bad. A very large percentage of patients in medical OPDs are suffering from psychic problems and out of these too the proportion of patients suffering from fake heart attacks and imagined cancer of various kinds is very high nowadays. Forty years back this was not the case. Psychic heart and cancer patients are especially vulnerable to feelings of helplessness and doom because of their inbuilt mental instability and they succumb to all type of fraudsters. These are the people then who are exploited by clever' heart specialists' and one sees innumerable cases of young healthy men who have been fitted with coronary (heart) stents for complaints purely psychological or neuromuscular. They are then put on prolonged heart blood vessel dilating drugs, which prescription is very difficult to change or modify because every succeeding doctor plays safe and continues the medicines out of fear of precipitating an attack by stopping it's medicines. This is so because no test or investigation despite the advanced technology which it is based on is or perhaps can be absolutely foolproof. After receiving a doubtful test result no one dares taking decisions based on his clinical judgement alone, no matter how high or well-versed he may be. And psychologically weak patients are masters in influencing test results in many ways by declaring development of pain and breathlessness etc. during stress tests, thereby casting shadow on other tests too. Earlier in my other book, *Leaking secrets) I have given example of a patient who was declared having no vessel problem on angiography but was nonetheless advised to continue his coronary dilating drugs at a major cardiology hospital in Delhi. The chief complaint of this patient was of a sensation of heaviness in left mammary area whenever he picked up his grand-daughter in his lap but no other load lifting would cause it. See how confidant were the cardiologists even after a costly angiography. This patient is in his eighties now and has by himself given up all heart medicines.

The moral of these words follows; every patient with complaints suggestive of coronary disease if not in a serious or moribund state must receive a comprehensive psychiatric examination before any costly or invasive testing or a stent insertion. This ought to be so by law like it is for sex determination in pregnant females. But will the vested interests of stent manufacturers and commission receivers allow that?

Chapter VIII

<u>LIFE-A LOVE STORY</u>

Looking back, I see that our life has been by and large an enjoyable journey, of course with many rough patches intervening. But we, me and my wife Bimla think of those difficult times as the salt and spice of life. The innate zest to live and a positive attitude which is a normal characteristic of youth helped us weather these. Bimla was never a complaining type and supported me at every twist and turn of times. We were both young and energetic and never lacked laughter and smiles even when there were tears in eyes. Chopping onion for salad?

In praise of youth: Anything old may be gold, as is said but youth is platinum and diamonds and much more. How many do remember Elizabeth Taylor- the famed actress of mid twentieth century, a model and personification of beauty when she was young and currant but with old age upon her, a withered and dry flower got mixed with dust 79 years old, with hardly anyone to mourn and feel for. Now talk of Marilyn Monroe, another sex symbol and a cultural icon. She lives and is remembered for her youth and charm even now. She lived and died in her blossom at 36, leaving an image and an example for a long time to come. Our own Maduballa, no less in any way also followed Marilyn dyeing at 36 in 1969 but continues to rule hearts even today. It is perhaps not very different for males also. One thing quixotic about old age deserves a mention and perhaps needs to be highlighted. While as one's physical capacity gets diminished with age, human desires continue to remain as ardent and active as in youth. This applies more to males than females especially with regard to sex. Males retain sexual desires and thinking, if not their prowess till quite late years-may be till early eighties. But there is a difference. The world appears very different when looked at through the sclerosed eyes of the old than when seen with youthful eyes. The latter add their own colour to it while as the old eyes have already exhausted their prowess. The world of the elderly is at best a hollow one, with hardly any action and when any old/bold man ventures 'Action' he is disgraced like one former chief of IMF, StraussKahn. He even lost his chance for French presidency. Perverted justice? Ungrateful progeny conspired? The French should have been wiser! They ought to have supported him? After all they have a reputation of being 'in love/bed all 24 hours' to uphold!

Have seniors lost their right to live and love? Why can't the mute multitude combine and move courts of justice against such violation of innate and basic human rights? Wakeup gentlemen, you have nothing to loose but your chains! Old bones are strong; Blast the greenhorns! How dare anyone deny value of experience? Now from grotesque to sublime:

A fond urdu poet, I don't remember his name, ardently prays to Allah in beautiful verse to let him die before any youthful lady can address him as 'Uncle'. This shows how lapse of youthful years and onset of later age is hated by those who know. Females fear loss of their youthful looks and attractiveness more than the males and even late age matrons don't shy away from painting themselves thick and their greying hair blonde or dark. Illusions too have value!
Remembering my own youth, while I have already related my initiation into my new life of love and

romance and how, as a measure of my 'great' wisdom, I considered myself an expert in matters of love, **I-a great love bird**, dare tell you a little more of my exploits.

Love affairs:In my second year at medical college, I initiated to stage a drama in the college premises. My professor of Anatomy who was fond of me encouraged me in this. But just a day or two prior to it's final on stage exhibition our female actress (Boys only had under university rules to act female roles also) got hospitalized for severe sickness and with no alternative in hand I took over the role of heroin in the drama. I was adjudged a good actor. In the process of holding rehearsals I had to contact the director of the drama both in my capacity as it' organizer and later as a lead actor also. He was a lecturer in anatomy and came from a high aristocratic family and often wanted me to talk to him on phone. As luck would have it, his sister would usually pick the phone and after enquiry would hand me over to him. I found her voice extremely sweet and charming and came to believe her to be equally attractive. So I started to phone them up very often both with or without adequate reason in order to be able to talk to her. I got mad to hear her and came to believe that she too was deeply in love with me, because she had by then come to recognize my voice and would hail me smiling whenever I phoned them up. Just my first word on the phone and she would say 'Yes, ganjoo, I knew.' These words were sweeter than honey in my ears and carried a deep and soul stirring message for me and I came to believe that she was as restless to talk to and to meet me as I was for her. It needs some effort and also great imagination on the part of those who are uninitiated in matters of love to appreciate how I spent the hours and minutes in between my telephone calls. I imagined her to be as much miserable as I was for her sake and that feeling worsened my pain and distress. I would have gladly volunteered to bear her portion of that love sickness; doubled and trebled in intensity, to make me wreathe and wriggle on my bed provided that kept her satisfied and cheerful. Nay I would have welcomed a jail sentence and even gallows if that would make her happy, but that could not be and that it was my misfortune tormenting her, I believed. Ah, how I wished some divine angel would come and inform me that she was happy and restful and did not suffer the pangs that tormented me. Sorrow and suffering should not lay even it's shadow on my beloved all her life; that was my most intense prayer. Time was slow and appeared heavy on me and I lay on my hostel bed turning and tossing, restless for the moment when my love would call to fix a meeting under that big baniyan tree that grew in their locality and was a source of cool shade to many in need of solace and comfort. Pain in my heart was of a wrenching character but it was very sweet also and more of it, I would not resent. My suffering was worse because I was suffering in silence, with my mouth tight shut. No one to console! How could I reveal my love tale to anyone else than her? The Baniyan tree also had it's own tale of love to tell me and I did believe it; every bit of it. It struck me perceptibly that everything around in this world was in love- 'mad love'. The baniyan tree was in love with the earth underneath it and it's aerial roots were hanging restless to meet that earth and to kiss it and clasp it fast and merge themselves into it inseparably. Themselves love-struck, the roots would be happy to accommodate we two impatient lovers; to give us refuge in their nest and then listen to our sweet dialogue in silence and learn some more of 'love techniques' from us to follow. And all three of us would be happy ever and ever after. Oh, it was sweet; just sweet! So days; my sweet days, went on and my restlessness knew no bounds. Sweet delirium! And then came the real zenith of my love story.

After we staged our drama on the D-day the actors were introduced to VIPs in the audience and we shook hands. Our director introduced us so and as I continued shaking hands I was introduced to a middle aged lady with a greying tuft of hair decorating her forehead as 'my sister Annapurna,' and a sweet known voice spoke to me, 'o I know him well. So you are ganjoo, very smart indeed,' I turned pale and kept gazing at her face. Beads of sweat appeared on my forehead and upper lip in that cold December night, as the director moved on and my lady also looked sideways unmindful of my misery. I felt weak and exhausted, my legs shaking. My fields of love watered with heart's blood abruptly washed off by Tsunami! World appeared crumbling around me.

It was difficult to believe that the episode was all a coinage of my own brain. Was it unreal that my fairy spoke love to me in that most melodious voice ever heard? How could I after all accept that the baniyan tree near their 'Haveli'(mansion) did not exist and did not offer it's cool shelter to us and did not promise by it's calm acceptance that we two shall live most happily in it's nest for ever and ever. Was the tree itself not in love? I swear I found it madly so. The wind and the sun and the moon were witness to it'secstasy.My innocent heart is a witness above all. What motive did I have to fabricate a story and suffer agony for days and wriggle in restlessness for nights on end? Was I mad to cheat my own self? I protest; I protest most vehemently. Ordinary earthlings can't imagine and won't believe that it really happened but I do in faith declare that all this actually happened to me and it was in paradise! Yes, it was in paradise.

Yet, yet, I feel sad to find that I had never actually visited the locality where my love lived and never seen with my eyes, her 'haveli' as also whether any baniyan tree grew near there. I wish I had checked the reality before having jumped headlong into that paradise. But it was sweet, worth dying for! Don't laugh please, because:

I can give a long list of my sweet follies, suffice it to say that one time I was madly in love with LataMangeshkar-the celebrated singer, also. Again I had imagined her to be as beautiful as was her voice and I intensely longed to see her in person. I used to get ecstatic forgetting the world around me while listening to her from radio Ceylon with her extremely beautiful face singing before my eyes. Oh, she appeared dazzling and as young and youthful as a fairy, all the time smiling and gesturing to me. Often I used to see her in my dreams flying in air as fairies are pictured in children's books, having wings. Her wings were made of music, so I thought and perhaps saw them in the dream as woven out of the famous song from 'Mahal' picture, 'Ayegaanewalla'. Retrospectively now, I can't understand how her wings were made out of a song but that time I would feel them so and saw them so. They were cream white in colour as was the said song.I actually felt and saw it so. Was I mad then or am I mad now?I let paradise slip out through my fingers repeatedly in my life, not just once. I am surely a great fool if not mad! Please don't laugh at me. But then came the news that TV had made it's appearance in America. I was full of joy but then my suspense and dismay grew because I could not understand how my beloved lata could come alive from a magnetic tape or a vinyl record that would be played at the TV station. There then followed a time when I saw her really singing on the TV screen but by then my brain fever had abated.

Some young children report vivid imagery of their thoughts and perhaps some artists also have it, but I am neither and so I have reason to believe in my love experiences as real. I am perhaps more closely related to our animal ancestors who are guided primarily by sense of hearing and smell than by sight and touch. Acute development of these two senses is vital to their survival in an open hostile environment. In my case, however, my sense of hearing led me often into vortexes of emotional storms and madness. I thank almighty for not having given me any chance to use my sense of smell that far. The results could have been catastrophic and you might have long back seen me duly handcuffed in pictures flashed across in newspapers; for pursuing and sniffing ladies at the wrong spot while they walked around. One can have some more idea about this perversion as also of the sense of taste, by reading of the

English opium merchant described in the novel 'Sea of poppies' by Amitav Gosh.

It may be interesting to note that sense of smell is very highly developed in certain animals and plays a very important role in their reproductive life beside providing for their survival. They smell a female to determine her time and suitability for mating. Thank God that humans have lost that primacy of smelling and senses of sight and touch have gained an upper hand. Were it otherwise we would also be smelling ladies and instead of saying 'She looks beautiful' we would declare 'She smells wonderful' and sniffing around would have been our primary occupation. But perhaps I at least would not make so many blunders as my ears led me to commit.

In the animal world females are available for mating only for a limited number of days of 'Heat' in a cycle but with human females without any restrictions of the kind and so fit for mating every time it would have been a very different, perhaps an interesting world; **'an amusement park', open 24x7x365.**Would the Indian parliament then have banned 'Smelling around' the way they have banned stalking? But the parliamentarians themselves would remain busy nosing beauties in Bollywood, Bombay. Freedom of thought, speech and above all 'Action' assured!

Indian men and Asians generally are not aware of the **importance of tallness and it's beauty**, in a lady. A tall lady is by nature intended to be beautiful and attractive irrespective of other feminine attributes that she may possess. Movement of her body parts especially of limbs and at waist with a greater range in geometrically symmetric proportion looks pleasing to the eye. Remember when Cleopatra enquires about Octavia's looks from her lady messenger the first in her list is 'How tall is she' and then about her colour (of skin) and finally about the shade of her hair and thereafter rests satisfied that Antony will not like her long. A tall pretty lady; a flower on a stalk! Our men give too much emphasis on a lady's skin colour not knowing the contribution which facial and body contours make in her attractiveness. A beautiful nose is for example a great asset in a beautiful face. Pascal was not a fool to have chosen Cleopatra's nose, of all her beauteous parts, for praise. He meant that and so said that. Persians considered **dimples on a face**signs of it's beauty and had elegant names for these. A dimple on cheeks while smiling was called 'Chahi-GubGub' a dimple on the chin was called 'ChahiZanakhdan'. 'Chah' in Persian meaning a pit. One of our highly placed professors would castigate north Indians for their rough skin. He praised Bengali and south Indian texture of skin for it's smoothness and blamed the north Indian skin roughness for it's 'mixed blood' origins; due to cross breeding with foreign invaders. But itemizing and separating beauty into it's parts is perhaps not a right thing to do. Beauty is beauty where ever you find it; it is just beautiful, or else a catalogue of it's bits will be unending. Haven't connoisseurs and lovers of beauty forgotten the killer eyes in the above index? The bravest and the mightiest are totally vanquished and devastated and volumes-full messages bombarded on their victim in seconds through them.

Bengali and south Indian beauties are indeed incomparable. Apart from their superb bodily features, dancing and music is in their heritage and in blood. Flat feet in a girl was considered a minus point for a girl at marriage time because these hindered quick movements in dancing. The lady medical student from Madras of dusky skin whom we described earlier is still before my eyes. Krishna had the same dusky shade of skin and Gopis are said to have been dying for him. Colour of a man's skin perhaps does not carry much significance but his qualities and position in life do.Vijyantimala, Sridevi, WahidaRehman, Jaya prada are but a few known names from the Hindi screen; all from south and every one was not actually fair. Suchitrasen once called 'the toast of Bengal' ruled hearts without discrimination. She had a typical Bengali shade of her skin. And of course our 'Carol' who was a lotus perhaps the lone one that blossomed in the orchard lake in Detroit, USA, begs description. Was she a nymph residing in the blue waters of that lake that had come to take me along to her abode as in folk tales, I wonder. I was 30 years of age then and she was 23. May she be well and happy where ever she may be! A glorious, sweet and delicious but heart rending memory!

But her and every **one's Beauty of mind** we did not talk about while talking of beauties of physic thus far. **Nature's packaging of goods is by far the best seen** and beautiful people are usually considered good and likeable people unless proved otherwise. The verse already quoted says 'when God bestows beauty, delicacy (of mind and action) joins in'. And this is perhaps summarized in the word 'Grace'. **Male or female, one must possess that God given grace** around. A graceful lady far transcends the descriptions of body contours and colour. She is joy itself.

A few words about our fascination with white colour of skin. Let us note that the colour of Indian's skin is not black but varies between wheatish brown to soft dark as talked about earlier in relation to our actresses or even Lord Krishna. Europeans, in particular the British and their relatives in their west would label us black out of contempt for a subjugated 'inferior race'. In comparison the Russians have a liking and softness for Indians as a whole and their skin colour no less. Mr. K.P.S. Menon, a reputed intellectual of his time and once our ambassador in soviet Russia tells his experience. His wife was admitted to a maternity hospital in Moscow for delivery. Meanwhile he was delivering a lecture somewhere and in between he was called to receive a telephone call. As he came back he sent the audience into peals of laughter by revealing, in his characteristic south Indian accent that it had been the maternity nurse saying 'Sir, your wife has delivered a 'beautiful black' female baby. Russia is geographically more in Asia and less in Europe and they like Indians and our culture.

We might as well say that white colour alone doesn't make a person beautiful and the fact is that most white women are just average as expected. Grace and 'class' appears wanting and eastern ladies score high in that. Many white ladies appear to have contracted some masculine traits through living hard competitive careworn lives perhaps. Females were not meant by nature to labour and live tense lives; that was reserved for the man hunter. There is a pretty saying in Bengali, "Lajja may dherabhushan" meaning 'shyness and a sense of shame; her blush, are a woman's ornaments'. These are perhaps lost amongst the white races. The two genders are treated as two fitting, complimentary parts of a machine that can generate fun for a change. The softer, poetic, humane and a lasting perception of love has been lost in both genders. Both Cleopatra and Helen of Troy were Eastern beauties and perhaps of brown-white Mediterranean skin colour.Grecian people apparently were fond of and would smuggle beautiful ladies from East Mediterranean coast; again of the same brown colour and their softer eastern features.Brown skin is appreciated and liked by many whites as appearing healthier and as a sign of vigour and virility and they go sun-tanning for the same reason. In fact white skin, green or blue eyes and blond hair are not original to Europe and came there from extreme north arctic coasts through barbarians called 'normans' when they invaded continental Europe and the entire race accepted the name of being of Nordic descent. White skin in them was due to mutations of melanin controlling genes developed in order to live under limited sunlight hours of their region. And now it may be time to go back to human sexual behavior:

Many females loose active interest in sex after menopause while in some there may a brief period of over yearning and interest for it at that juncture of life, so to say the last flicker of brightness. Some loose all interest in the activity just after the first child birth and many are totally ignorant about climactic pleasure called orgasm that occurs after strenuous activity involved in mating. Women who learn about orgasm from books or from friends but in actuality don't experience it themselves, either blame their own physiology for it or blame their man for underperformance. In the latter case the results may not be wholesome for the social unit as she may start looking around for that elusive experience only to feel more disappointed and unhappy. Such females are often described as 'Frigid'.

As earlier pointed out loving and love making can be a soul elevating experience involving some feelings of homage service and surrender to the good qualities of the beloved and a wish to sacrifice oneself for that. It is commonly said 'so and so is dying for her'. This has a profound psychological meaning. You look at your partner or talk to him/her and somehow feel delighted and attracted, want to come closer and touch to feel the beloved and many people feel like merging with the pleasing beloved and so get involved in actual love making. One can and does sacrifice many things dear for a love, even may be one's life if occasion so arises. So love making is not all selfish gratification or aggression (in males) or tolerance or masochism in females as is said. It is a mixture suited to and determined by circumstances and one's mental cultivation. Many ladies have a psychological resistance or bloc against surrender of their selves; their ego in love making and this could be causative of their frigidity. Real enjoyment in mating perhaps comes from letting oneself go and even perhaps vanish in that evolving sense of enjoyment and happiness in union. Ladies seem to be particularly vulnerable to distortions at this stage and hence their so called frigidness. It is common observation that a lady looses interest in coitus at the slightest noise that occurs then or a fear for example, that a door is left unbolted and someone may come in, etc. Treatment of frigidity has to be psychological primarily.

During early phases of biological evolution, reproduction of organisms took place by asexual division of cells. It took nature millions of year of trial and error to develop this sexual type of reproduction. Apart from other benefits it's greatest benefit has been a rapid development of intelligence which has among humans reached it's zenith so far. Our power of making concepts and our emotional life processes are the most developed. It is this emotional life and it's working that is important in our love making. As pointed out already, human love and love making are central to self-actuation, self-realization and identity consolidation. The growing adolescent comes to know himself through exposure to hetro-sexual love and is finally reminded of his position in life and the rights and responsibilities that go with it by the same heterosexual interests, it's demands and later contacts. In short man locates himself in life by virtue of his sexual orientation and this also furthers his intellectual growth as well as grasp. Central place of sex in animal life is recognized by nature in providing the incentive of highest order viz., feeling of joy and pleasure of orgasmic intensity and proportions at it's accomplishment. The only purpose behind our creation by nature is to continue life's process through continuation of species. **And love life plays a fundamental role.** A rich love(emotional) life is a rich cultural life; a life of lights and colours, of lyrics and poems, of Shakespearean like living pulsatingdramas,and Ghalib's like love soaked quotes and couplets, of people young at heart. It is a life rich in arts and of everything beautiful and optimistic. It is a life rich in imagination and thought. And in the very meaning of life. And that is joy- a serene joy the **joy and happiness of love.**

A foul manifestation of love making is rape. It is all beastly aggression which human beings are in no way devoid of. Aggression is essentially a masculine quality and determines many things good for humanity when sublimated or converted, which a cultivated mind is trained to do from early days of life. In rapes combined with harm to or murder of the victim it is naked untamed aggression plus a vengeance for the opposite sex that are responsible for the crime. The latter could be determined by the perpetrator's early life development and events. It is the same aggressive sex impulses when tamed and transformed that bloom into poetry, art or music and general human development and when not sublimated can cause crimes, rapes and murders. Similarly, masochism or the spirit of tolerance is essentially a female trait but is found in needed proportions in males too, as was said earlier that we are all bisexual.

Sadism (Aggressiveness) and masochism vary in intensity and manifestation, as is said in the two genders but in the same gender and in the same person too with one's age and circumstances. Hence we see dynamic and forthright and even harsh men turning sweet and lovable in their later years, their rough edges get smoothened with age as if. Conversely many soft and sweet ladies grow moustaches and facial hair, more on their chins, needing regular removal coupled with a visible change in their temperament. Their sweet voice turns harsh and manly and words spoken by them acquire signs of authority and command much to the discomfort of their poor husbands. The latter, even those that were strong and authoritarian in their younger days often run for cover. Orders must be obeyed! Often such female matrons exercise complete authority over the whole household, nay, over the whole country and the world stands amazed. I remember our Indira Gandhi, Margaret Thatcher, Golda meiretc etc. Indiraji was a coy, sublime, unassertive and unassuming beautiful lady at her prime who turned into The iron lady of India as she matured. Army generals would quiver and crawl in her presence. **And now on to sex education for children** because this in my opinion is not desirable. We are writing here about how to remain joyful in life, so let us not kill the joy of innocence amongst our young ones. Don't turn them into 'Grown-ups' too early'

The words and the concept sound truly modern and typically American and so our political leaders many of them illiterate, are enamoured of it. One thing to be asked about it is; has sex education benefitted people in advanced countries and if so in what way. The answer is a positive 'No'.Generalized courses in the subject can be damaging to immature minds that are forced to know what they have no use for. It arouses undue curiosity in them about a topic which many may not have ever even thought of.Yes, most children have doubts/questions about how babies are born and about the intimate relations between their parents etc, but these are things which the child gradually solves himself with time. They have questions about many things non- sexual also like the sun, moon and how and why it rains etc. But these too are solved in time through many natural unadvertised ways. Why is sexual education only given so much emphasis? Perhaps because talking about it pleases the adult advisors themselves. Has introduction of this education reduced tensions in those adults who received it in school days? Has it decreased the incidence of mental disease in advanced countries? No! Mental disorders and strife are on the increase in all western countries and in America.

On the other hand, increased curiosity at a young age leads and has led to increased experimentation in the subject at an inappropriate age resulting in teen age sex and teen age pregnancies. In India which is already ridden with problems of all kinds this one also will need to be added to the list. As a psychiatrist, I have failed to understand what needs to be taught to youngsters on a mass scale about sex and in what way does an average child feel handicapped for want of that knowledge. Individual children may have troubling doubts about some aspects ofsex but these should be solved for them only at an individual level and not generalized for the whole class. Such dissemination of un-needed knowledge can create anxiety in children who otherwise never thought of such questions as may be troubling some individual child. This unwanted and undigested knowledge can distract children in their studies and some may even start spying on their parents and near relatives in order to gain full knowledge on the interesting topic. We are basically humanized animals and who teaches our brethren amongst other animal races what to do about mating. Every one finds his own path under the impulse of the inborn instinct. Nature needs no human guidance. Those who develop troubling doubts about sex early in life, should surely be helped to solve their problems but later also, such children may need to be monitored for grosser mental problems for which they may as well be candidates.

Children get their best schooling on sex matters at home where between the ages of two to five they go through what is called 'Oedipus complex' and by resolving this they acquire their gender roles and in years to follow they identify with one of the parents or parent substitutes and unconsciously keep learning things. Later effect of seeing pet and domestic animals as also stray ones, engaged in mating raises curiosity perhaps of a pleasing kind but no grave concerns. Where ever a child feels over concerned with this matter of fact learning he should be helped but not every child needs help for this. After 10 or 11 years the adolescent has his peers to teach him what is really needed for his stage of life and nothing more and the process continues in this natural manner till adult hood is reached. Meanwhile masturbatory activity with adult type phantasy accompanying automatically develops and that helps towards the ultimate goal of finding actual object relationships. The most important period of learning in the process is that which the child traverses uptill the age of 5 or 6 years and this forms the foundation not only for one's sex activity but for the whole life activity later. Unnecessary interference with a natural process can have adverse effects for the child and later on for the society, as is happening in the west, where people are made to think of everything and every event in terms sexual. What was a taboo earlier has been made a fashion So a shoe can be 'Sexy', hair creams and soaps are naturally sexy, design of your house sexy and soon bricks and stones used therein will be termed sexy? It seems the use of the word 'sexy' pleases every one and is not objected to but encouraged. That veil of secrecy and shame about sex having been lifted overnight, an overreaction is observable and this may not be well in all matters. That innate poetic sense and humour of a basic kind which is present in even the ordinary person and that inborn abstract conception of human love is attempted to be presented in concrete form and terms, while aesthetic sense even in mutual relations is likely to get obliterated. Even Bertrand Russell agrees that availability of easy sexual outlets can make poetic or artistic talent of a potential poet or artist unnecessary. A cordial and friendly hand shake can confirm a business deal while some slight deviation in holding the offered hand may announce it's doom; a hand shake with a lady prolonged by a few seconds makes a world of difference. Thousands of messages have been carried either way, unknown to you and me. Differences of very fine character in human communications and their varying nuances have to be accepted as vital in the conduct of a natural and meaningful life or else our lives face the risk of getting totally mechanical and everything we do or think or feel will come to be measured by the scale and tested in the laboratory. And that will be the end of humanity per se though humans may continue their mechanical existence on the planet. The difference between a wife and a sister may, if things so continue, be explained in scientifically verifiable anatomical terms only. Hay! we are living in a scientific age where no superstition will be tolerated.

ANEXAMPLE: I remember an incident from my school days when I was around ten years of age. There lived a sweetmeat shop owner by name 'ZindaHalwai' in the neighbourhood of our school. He was a thick set fair young man in whom his youth appeared to be specially showing itself, by way of an active temperament, joviality and a shining pair of eyes. His curly jet black hair, were long enough for attention but appeared more attractive and shinning after his daily bath when he would oil them freely and let them loose without combing. Instead of using his hand to swipe those away from his eyes and face he would jerk his head to throw them backwards. This mannerism looked good on him and he was apparently conscious of that as of his flourishing youth. Closer still than Zinda's shop was a house with a high wall around it, just across the street from our school where there lived a young married woman by name Sa---.We had never seen her husband but saw the lady often looking out of one of their windows. The house several times drew our attention when Zinda was seen during our mid-day recess, climb it's wall and then walking tight rope walk on it's edge to reach a window which all the boys knew to be of her room and then jump in. Peace at last! His bowed but strong shiny muscular legs visible in shorts during summer months served him well. Benefits of variety? Wise men know it! We in any case didn't know nor did we bother our brains to speculate his business in doing so, but it gave us much pleasure and reason for laughter to see Zinda going into that room and the matter would end there for us with the school bell ringing. It had absolutely no other meaning in our mind except that the ever jovial Zinda was entering that lady's room through a window instead of a door and we never cared whether her husband or the other members of their large family were there those times or not. Now please put this story before a ten or eleven-year-old in present times and he will illuminate you on that business of Zinda brilliantly. He already stands informed about such adult interests through his mobile and the computer. So what do our sex educators want to educate him more about? And what have people of earlier generations lost by not attending formal classes on sex?

CHAPTER IX

<u>AIM OF LIFE</u>

There was a time when psychoanalysis was being blamed for involving sex in everything it talked of but now the same psychoanalysis blames this world for doing the same thing with the worst kind of understanding and usage of the same sex. We accept that the bright sun invigorates and sustains the myriad forms of existence, both animate and inanimate in this world. But we don't confuse and equate the sun with for example an ordinary plant that grows in the garden by dint of the sun's light. Similarly, we declare that there is a myriad form of expression of our sexual instinct each of which may look and behave as different as earth is from the sun, nonetheless, their existence and maintenance is from the sexual instinct. Take the case of a scientist who spends all his time in his laboratory neglecting his wife and family as well as the rest of the world in pursuit of his researches. In the lay language it will be said that professor so and so is totally wedded to his studies/research. Is that wrong to say so? We say that he has sublimated his sexual aggressive impulses and diverted his libido into socially useful and productive channels. A rough mechanical (scientific) minded person of today may as well say that the professor's research is 'sexy' and that is why he is after it. There is a difference of understanding. We recognize maternal love, love of a sister, a child, a father or mother and one's wife as absolutely different forms of love yet all are derived from the same root of sexual instinct which is born with us at our birth and does not fly into us at adolescence as is believed by other 'scientific' people.

Love of an unattainable lady flowers into a glorious poem on the lips of her lover; how should one explain it else than the poet has sublimated his sexual urges into a wonderful poem. The world is richer thereby. And that is why we say that under the progress of humanity lies the hand of our sexual instinct modified so as to be useful to others. How else should one explain the romantic poems of the earlier referred to poetess 'HabbaKhatoon' when she openly asks for her beloved to come and enjoy her garden of youth which she says is in full bloom, after she lost him. It will be lengthy to explain that more than three fourth of human thinking and behavior is directly or indirectly influenced by or is completely dependant on or derived from a transformed and sublimated sex instinct, but it is immodest and crude to declare that all this activity happens because of genital sex and that is what is attempted to be done by promoters of all things sexy. Similarly, the other one fourth of human development is traceable to our instinct of self-preservation including that of hunger etc. And hence we have our fine restaurants and hotels and food and wine industries; every third or fourth shop in your locality caters directly or indirectly to this instinct. I must remind my youngsters that the most beautiful and the most fragrant flower in life is **the flower of romance** and it is really unfortunate of those who have instead of enjoying it's charms taken the shorter, so called American route to enjoyment by resorting to quick sexual satisfaction. That crude path belongs to rapists and the shallow among the humans. Swine feed on the refuse and relish the garbage. For humans no better words than from Gurudev Tagore: Romantic love gives you a spring full of bright colourful flowers and leaves behind an autumn of delicious and sweet memories.

AIM OF LIFE;We had earlier declared that life appears an aimless, purposeless lapse of time in the life-span of an animal. But, why of an animal only? The entire sentient as well as the non-sentient world appears treading the same path.From the very start of universe with the big bang through the start of life in the primordial soup toit's final evolution into the cosmos as we see and understand it today everything appears going on aimlessly and purposelessly though completely in an orderly and predictable manner. But, tell this to any religious zealot and he will swear that we have been bestowed this invaluable life to meet God and to go to heaven to enjoy with 72 Hurs there. Even this madcap has an aim for his life howsoever absurd that may be.Tell it to a person in love, he will vehemently deny the purposelessness of his life. He has actually seen his purpose with his eyes, felt it in his heart throbs and his brain is still reeling under it's impact. He has tasted ecstasy in reality; he is ready to face hell but not give in. How dare you call his love unreal, he asks! Tell a father who is busy collecting money, rupee by rupee, for his children's school fees to be paid next month and he declares the aim of his life to get the best education for his children. He insures his life in order to fulfill his aim/bondage even in his possible death. At the same time, by insuring his life he has, never mind, most foolishly made his own life redundant and useless to the same children whose future he is constantly worried about. Tell any nature lover that the beauty of his hills and mountains or my own beloved leopard is unreal and useless and we will join to call any one so saying, bull headed and so on and so forth. Every one of them, nay, every one of us has a reason and purpose to be alive.

And that is the crux of the matter! And it's solution too. All these so called sensible people have filled up the vacancy and valuelessness of their life with a value;

given it a purpose and a direction which no scientific discovery or invention can negate. It may ultimately be immaterial whether that direction and aim was right or wrong but it's presence in some form or the other appears necessary. The psychic dimension of our life, which we earlier called the 'fourth dimension', keeps continuously asking for it. This gives man his identity and belongingness. Something or some person must belong to you or you to that thing or person. In short you develop an active interest in that something, which may be any individual, an animal, a garden, building or even books or something as insubstantial as an idea or a philosophy. You become it's votary or supporter and conversely that supports you unconsciously. And now you come to live for something.

The reader might have wondered why the author in his musing (as he calls it) goes round and round to finally zero in on the subject of females mostly. And I reply: Please peep into your own heart (better ask for an analyst's services) and then ponder: Why did the creator find it necessary to create Eve to accompany Adam? She is that 'something', that man lives for most of his life, and she is 'The joy in life' which he seeks consciously or otherwise. Please remember the word 'Misfortune' used by Bertrand Russell (Already quoted) to describe a state where any man may remain ignorant of this bliss of life. **To enjoy this bliss unknowingly is different from 'celebrating' it in the glow of it's knowledge and consciousness.** And that is what I wish the reader to know. It has a different charm then and one feels that life has been a gainful employment; not useless and purposeless!

Somerset Maugham in his brilliant novel 'Of human bondage' states that even creation of a piece of lawn and it's maintenance may become a purpose in one's life. It can become no less than a Taj Mahal for an average person, if created with that dedication. It becomes a bond or better still 'a bondage' in life; similar things are marriage and one's family etc. It is not for fun and enjoyment alone that people should marry and have children, because in turn it involves much botheration too. It is a tragedy of our times to loose sight of the real significance of marriage and there are intellectuals who deride this institution as unnecessary and an encumbrance in life. Life is thought of as something that should yield continuous pleasure and thrills only. Such expectations give disappointments as their natural corollary and divorces follow as quickly in the hope that the new partner will give renewed pleasure. The joy of a sustained marriage and the family is of a different but lasting nature it is 'delicious'; even the pains that accompany this enterprise are delicious. Your child admitted to a hospital in serious state is an extremely painful situation to you but that pain is truly delicious; you would like to incur more of that pain if it helps your child to recover a little. The same in case of your wife who after a few years of cohabitation has come to be a close friend and confident of your's. You will not hesitate to give your blood for her or even your extra kidney for her survival and she for your's. All this involves pain but it is a sweet pain that you volunteer for gladly and remain proud of that for all time. 'Fourth dimension' of human life seeks bonds and roots for itself like it seeks a purpose or aim in life and that is why the **tradition of marriage** exists. Family is a secure bond; one gets rooted in it. Marriage involves much sacrifice but that is truly enjoyable because it helps you to dig your roots more firmly in life and give it a purpose. Of all the animal species, mammals who are the last evolved have an inborn instinct of caring for their children and suckling them with mammae etc. Amongst humans this instinct is the most developed in caring for their new borns for a very long time. It is natural in us and hence a source of pleasure which advocates of 'No marriage, no bondage; only quick thrills' theory, do not understand. In later life when grown up children fly away, parents feel an emptiness around; a situation called 'the empty nest syndrome', and life feels purposeless unless the aged persons can rely on some alternative bonds like in friends, close relatives, some religiosity even when we know that the latter is all a superstition and make-believe only, books etc not money please. On the contrary spending it away to render some help to, say, a poor relative of your's can rebound on you in the form of a feeling of great achievement and satisfaction at least. You can be assured of a v. good compensation. Arrangements for that are well laid out already. Earlier started/done the better it proves.

Aged persons need somehow to make themselves useful, at least to their own selves. A mix of religion, yoga, books and nature love can be a good plan. It must be realized that idleness makes one's life 'idle' and purposeless. It can eat at the 'charm' that were your earlier times. Hence please try to remain attached to your earlier occupation as much as you can and as much as your circumstances allow. For example, a shopkeeper should not give up sitting at his shop merely because he has come of age and feels weak or has body pains. Idleness will cure neither. A retired employee should take up some suitable engagement and keep earning up to the last. He can donate his earnings to some poorer relative and that way gain love and respect of others. Independence and self-assertion that he gains thereby will add pleasure and purpose to his life. Activity can add charm to days. I ask my aged lady patients also to keep their arms and legs working till the last even when their daughters in law are at hand. They should never give up at least their governance of the home even on a sick bed. That keeps their interests alive. (I see a daughter in law smiling to herself at my words) Grandchildren are a great asset to invest in; the sweetest fruit you can taste in this season of life. But try not to depend on any one.

In short, one would say that one must give oneself a cause for which to live. Great people, one can see, have succeeded in doing so. Great revolutionaries and reformers and leaders, it is said, have lived for a cause. Lenin lived for the revolution and felt 'called upon' for it's sake. Hitler with all his madness of anti-Semitism (he didn't suffer it alone; the entire Christian world was replete with it) was solid in his patriotic belief that he was a man of destiny and after a failed assassination attempt on him, declared his firm belief that his cause was correct and that nature had saved him in order that he complete his mission. Socialist revolutionaries from lenin to Che Guevara put their limb, life and liberty at stake for the sake of their dear cause. Russian revolutionaries kept themselves ever ready for exile to Siberian wilderness. They had a cause! Cause gives meaning to life and meaning gives satisfaction and thereby happiness to it. Great men may have great causes for themselves to live for but small causes of small men can be and surely are no less great in meaning and effect. As already hinted, each one of us is and should feel himself a king. Give yourself a cause. You can be sure it will turn out a great kingly cause.

It is pathological to try to obliterate/deny your early life memories just because many of these are coloured in flamboyant colours and even have an erotic tinge. So these may conflict with your later-age 'assumed' religiosity and the-other-wordliness. See what Tolstoy has to say about the deliciousness of those childhood memories, their naughtiness, mischievousness- 'Natkhatpan' which you too have had in plenty. Remember those times and you will have plenty of reason to smile and laugh at your own self. "life was not a waste" you will agree with yourself. Youth and early adulthood of most people is not entirely barren. The colourful flowers that came your ways then, the friendships you developed, your-then world of imagination and it's accompanying heart throbs, those killer disappointments that killed you so often as well as the sweet pain of thorns that bruised you while collecting the blossom of that age, please remember those moments and you will again say "life was well spent". Still later, one day in a thoughtful moment you will reminisce with yourself 'My two children are well educated; employed fruitfully and by and large adjusted. Both of us (wife and myself) are keeping good health.

Oar's was an arranged marriage; just two unknown people meeting and it is so strange and unexplainable how we have got so close. We feel actually like one only, or at least feel like living for each other only! We have had wonderful moments together and the enjoyment that we had then, I don't think anyone else could have ever had more. It was just sweet and it is no less delicious now. We have constructed our own house with a small thumb-nail sized lawn in front and an equally large piece for kitchen garden at back. These keep both of us busy mentally as well as physically. She supplies a portion of our veg. requirements from her kitchen garden and they taste more delicious than what we buy from market. I have enough savings for rainy days and old age and also the children are obedient and loveful and caring. All of us together, we are so happy and everyone enjoys moments of togetherness. Their marriage should be no problem; let them decide about that themselves and let them take their time. We are by and large comfortably placed; no botherations, happy! We have had our share of difficult moments, in fact plenty of them but we have crossed over. People are not every time good but there is no dearth of good men also. Many people have helped me so often and I am here. I have no regrets about not collecting riches and all that goes with those and as some people in my knowledge have acquired, by foul means and fair. Their riches to them and life's happiness to me. I am contented with what I have and don't feel any need. That old Persian saying "my life's enjoyments have been no less than the Sultan's" will come to your mind. Life has been a good excursion and useful too. Thank god!' And you will again smile to yourself.

You are also reminded that you, all your life was noble and good. And never felt bad about other's-your relative's and neighbor's acquisitions or affluence and that you were never jealous of anyone. And that has been my nature from the very start. you will recollect. Wrong, categorically wrong, Sir! Man is by nature, like all animals jealous, jealous of everything that others possess, even when he himself is cast and immersed in plenty. Look at small children. It is a habit with them to survey the food plates of other children in a group and automatically compare what has been given to others with his own plate. Sibling rivalry is a well-known phenomenon, one is jealous of one's own brothers and sisters automatically from early age. Often, it is said, one is not as distressed by what he does not possess as by seeing his relatives and neighbours possess that. So you could not have been that noble and that different from the average person. Yes, gentleman, you have achieved something great; you have curbed your animal tendencies, without noticing what a great feat you were attempting all your life. It is just a matter of practice-(Abhiyas).Gradually teach yourself something new. Something that helps you to stay calm and happy in life.; look towards your own self and never compare. It takes time to develop this attitude and it automatically reinforces itself with it's results. You realize that you stay happier without bothering about others. Greek philosopher Epicurus advised his followers live a modest life. Moderation in life is a way to happiness. Flaunting one's riches and an ostentatious life style can become a cause for your own unhappiness as well as for those around you!

 Religion perhaps has it's own place in life but I have a grievance: It has by and large discouraged 'celebration' of life in "This world", asking men to wait for 'Hurs'and 'the plenty' in the "next".The concept of 'Sin' is a mischief and a fraud played on human happiness.Ethics and morality are not dependent on this.Atheists can be and many are very good 'men'and it is a great achievement in life to be a good 'man'.This theory of sin is indeed a creature of sinful and morose minds.

I once happened to visit a 79 year old lady who had multiple 'arthritic'(a part of her psychological malady) problems and pains had made her life a hell.She slept very little and ate still less and would weep for little reasons.Constantly she would repeat that she was being punished for her past sins.Asked for details she replied 'youthful follies, who is free from that;I had forgotten God then'.Just to pep her up I told her, 'you must have been very pretty then'.She replied, 'And that is what I am paying for now and then this, this my age'. I continued, my grand-father lived full 99 years so happily and a quick retort came "Tobah,Tobah"(God forbid, God forbid).Life had at that age become unbearable for her with the weight of her 'sins'.A clear picture of clinical Depression!

She felt a lot better with treatment and her so called arthritic pains were mostly relieved with a good sleep added.This is what can happen with cultivating wrong attitudes towards one's life.

Brothers and sisters, live life as it comes to you. Some tend to take it seriously; money, riches and power become their only aim of life. That life could have been a happy tale of the possible to be realized in actuality, is forgotten. And as a reaction formation to this stupidity and the guilt over unscrupulous deals of life, fruitless but trumpeted religious rituals and prayers are undertaken. Excessive religiosity is an attempt to regain lost pleasures in the other world. It also helps to wash off their load of guilt and they feel pious thereby.

I am surprised by the way people chant god's name ad-
nauseumor keep repeating passages from scriptures day
in and day out, in order to please him by showing their
love for him. Is that a correct method of showing one's
love for one's beloved? Suppose one of your own close
ones starts shouting or even whispering 'I love you,I
love you, forgive my sins, forgive my sins, make me the
richest man here. Iwant to purchase that seven storey
building and silence my jealous relatives and neighbours
once for all etc.' in your ear continuously, what will
happen to you? You will either take him to the nearest
psychiatrist or yourself turn mad and be taken there.
Similarly, I believe if there ever existed a God he must
have turned mad long back with such global chants
ringing in his ears all the time or at least turned stone
deaf by the sound of bells gongs, drums and shouting
over loud speakers long ago. Or else if that beloved is
omniscient like what our god is supposed to be, won't he
know our fake or true love for him without having to be
bored by our continuous chants? Also won't he instead
retort by asking as to how we are looking after and
tending to the work he had started, and how if at all we
loved him did we copy and continue his example in
deed? And will he not silently wonder at our duplicity
and cheating and accept us to have gone mad due to
excessive greed?

We are also very clever, mind you. Going to a temple or any place of worship, we offer a small sum of money say Rs: 101/- or some other 'token of love' to the deity while asking for that 'seven storied building', promising to come back with double that sum etc., when he gets us 'the building'. Is God a fool also?

O, He had dreamt a dream and planned and planted a garden, a paradise upon this earth with it's lush forests, singing streams of clean and clear waters, it's crystal clear sweet water lakes, it's green meadows and flower beds, fields and fruit trees spread all over. It was so planned that it would suffice all the genuine needs of it's inhabitants but he had not calculated for human greed. See what have we made of it? Look to the jungles of concrete-your cities are, all the artificiality of our lives, that pristine air and water all turned foul. The atmosphere, in his world was once so silent and peace giving but now is full of noise and irritation. Did/do we care for his method and intention? Yet we brazenly shout 'I love you, I love you'. Will our chanting and bead counting work?

 One would suggest trying not to harm anyone or anything around in this garden; that will be against human ethics as well as morality. It is a paradox that an ordinary human being has little power to do good but harm he can easily. Widespread vanity amongst men (ego problem) about their individual greatness and goodness prevents this realization. It is seldom realized that even the morsel that one consumes is basically snatched from someone else's mouth at least theoretically. So let us be careful but no 'sins' theory please! To err is human and every one of us can and does err. Don't seek forgiveness from the skies but try to correct yourself. If possible apologise to the wronged person with an open heart. He will feel good about it and you will feel relaxed; one tension less!

To sum up it can be said that a life well rooted and with a purpose in view, right or wrong no matter, is usually a peaceful life.

Maugham compares life to a Persian carpet whereof each thread, each knot, each colour has it's important role in the whole make and even a drunkard poet as also a lady prostitute is declared as having a purpose in the tapestry of life. The drunkard, he says, 'was his own justification'. Our life is described as a play of 'moonbeams'; weave them as you can and as you please. In this world of relative existence one brick has a use and purpose only in relation to another brick; mutual bondage determines their usefulness or otherwise. Nagarjuna the Indian philosopher far earlier, reached the same conclusions in his doctrine of 'Shunyata' (nothingness). (Read 'Maya'ofadvaita Vedanta). Self-satisfaction and one's own pleasure are the yard sticks of quality in life and it's purpose. That is what justifies it! Let others say what they have to!

Now I don't think it will be unreasonable to say that this principle of relative existence doesn't   limit itself to our relations with each other only but extends to every bit and part of our individual bodies and personalities also. Our lungs don't need to breathe for themselves nor does our heart pump blood for itself; kidneys don't filter poisons out for their own purpose. They are acting in relation to and for the sake of the rest of body. I would emphasize, they are working in order to serve our brain. In fact, what we have earlier called the 'Scaffolding' is all existing in the service of our brain. But that is not where it all stops. The brain is working in relation to and in the service of our consciousness which is a vast realm-a universe in itself. And in this vast universe of consciousness, is tucked somewhere a miniaturized super-computer called the 'MIND'. And that is what we have been talking about-this 'maharaja' of humanity, everything in it's service, in short. This maharaja in turn keeps a strict watch over all his employees and even whips them to regularity and constant work. And if you want to keep this 'maharaja' cheerful and peaceful, do take care of his servants i.e. your body organs that serve it. Keep them fit to serve your mind well. That is why I have detailed the exercises for your heart and lungs and brain in detail, earlier. A fit body keeps a cheerful mind! Out of all the vital organs that serve the consciousness, please note that there is only one consciously moveable and directly exercisable organ and that is our lungs. And coupled with heart these are most central and crucial to our health and life. Fortunately, any exercise of lungs is automatically an exercise of the heart and indirectly of the brain also. Slow deep breathing in time of stress immediately calms your nerves. This is then the key to health of other organs too. Hence the importance of breathing exercises in maintaining a healthy consciousness and a healthy mind/ memory function. Most doctors are trained to diagnose and treat diseases only; they never attend to diagnosis of positive health and to promote that.

A few words about usefulness of money in life: Generally, money is needed only to provide for day to day run of life and as a security for the rainy day, including old age and illness. There has to be a limit for both and that must be reasonable. It was reported that a lady actress turned politician who ultimately became a chief minister, beside untold wealth, had collected thousands of shoes and sandals, thousands of wrist watches and uncountable number of saris and dress wear. Is that a sensible thing to do? But most of us do it, in our own way depending on one's reach and resources. But no one can have use for or consume things/money beyond a limit even if one decides intentionally to do so. Thereafter starts the process of hoarding fueled by more and more greed for which there is no limit. One wishes those un/fortunate people who are in the business of building empires and treasures 'somehow', were also happy at heart. Unfortunately, most are not! It is an ordinary fact but not noticed that use as well as 'need' of money changes with one's stage of life. For a small boy, a wad of notes can be a good play material; the same boy in the college later will be surprised if suddenly granted a wad of 2000 rupee notes and may pick one or two out of the bundle to enjoy his fast foods with his friends that day. For the rest of money, he will happily thank you and run away. The same boy gradually learns that to possess big money makes a 'big man' and then he too joins the scramble. Come late years, the same boy now an elderly man if given 'big' money says 'what shall I do with so much, give it to my sons, they need it'. Money obviously has no intrinsic value of it's own, it is all how important you take it. Our thinking and attitudes determine it's value. And that is what is needed to change for a happier life. In Hinduism there is a hymn, called 'Gayatri mantra', which every believer is supposed to chant, first thing in morning. It is to ask for 'Budhi', meaning reason and discrimination. Not for wealth and riches! If one has the right 'budhi' everything rightly needed will follow. Almost all religions are unanimous in this belief.

One does not have to be a Hindu or even learn Gayatri mantra for seeking reason and discrimination, as said. Simply one can meditate in silence for a short while any time of the day and 'remember' that one needs 'peace of mind' the most. Meditation? <u>Remember your God? NO, please.</u> He perhaps does not exist and even if he did exist our attempt should be not to ask for outside help. Development of self will and self-confidence is the aim of this exercise. That grants peace. Just ask yourself to be calm and patient while you concentrate on your breathing. Simply ask yourself to remain peaceful; attempting to control your mind is the aim. You may whisper 'Peace' or 'I want peace', as you like. But 'Om shanti I find is a better and a meaningful phrase for this purpose. 'Om' basically is a secular two syllable sound and I don't know if it has any meaning. It is of all the unintelligible sounds one that can be lengthened or shortened as the situation needs. Hindu Rishis have apparently researched well on this. Controlled deep slow breathing will help you to relax immediately and restlessness of mind will also decrease. Long in-breathing is accompanied by the sound of O.......m, lengthened as needed, to be followed by an equally long sound 'Shanti'or 'Peace'. Please note that OM does not refer to any God or should not be confused with any religious symbol. It has come to be uttered before the start of any work by Hindus and is simply like 'Bismilla' in Arabic(in the name of God) considered auspicious. Let me repeat it that the sound 'Om' is not owned or patented by Hindus and being totally unconnected with any Hindu God is a completely secular non-religious sound and no one should object to it's use. We have no objection if someone replaces it with 'Bismillah' but that might prove elaborate and hence not suitable. Even otherwise the attempt has to be on developing one's own confidence and so involving God in any manner may be counter-productive.

 Back to breathing exercise; you will find that you will gradually become a calm person internally. Peace will dawn!

Neither ask for peace nor riches not even for forgiveness for sins from outside or from someone sitting in the skies; It is all inside you. Please remember the famed Persian Sufi poet Hafiz quoted earlier when he says that you yourself are the god. Self-confidence is what is needed to generate peace of mind. And peace of mind automatically gives discrimination and the two combined grant an internal joy and self-satisfaction. I remember a famous Kashmiri poet namely Mehjoor, who says 'I want this, this and this; also I needed that, that and that. Alak, alak! I didn't know what I really needed. It was peace of mind that I needed the most! Give me a restful heart somehow. Please!

One often finds sponsored newspaper columns by economists advising people to invest in mutual funds so as to create a corpus of a crore or more to ensure a comfortable life in old age and unfortunately young literate wage earners fall in this trap mostly. These people have no feel of actual life. And then economics is hardly a science. It is not even an art. The former demands precision and the latter perfection Itis just statistical jugglery, as in/exact as is astrology and it's predictions just that fabled midwife's promise of 'either a boy or a girl' kind. Can any one of them give us the exact undisputed cause of great depression even after ninety years of it's happening? One does not have to call them all the names that John Perkins himself an economist of world repute calls them in his best-seller 'the Hitman'. The name itself suffices to explain and describe much about them. But one is reminded of a 'hitman' nearby, in India, lately. Leaving aside his jugglery of economics Mr.Amrityasen, an India born American economist, has hit the culture of this country most ignobly. He has declared that Lord Rama has never been a part of Bengali culture/religion. This, as expected, to please the ruling clique there. Ask him the name of the principal secular saint of Bengal and of India please. It begins with Rama to end with Krishna. He was the teacher of our national saint-philosopher, Swami Vivekananda. Krittivasi Ramayana in Bangla composed in 14th century could have taught the American-bred 'Hitman' about history as well as the conditions(economics)of Bengal then.Instead of knowing facts from a half dozen Bangla Ramayanas that exist, he has got his knowledge, as per his own words, from his 4th grade convent studying granddaughter. But that is how 'hitmen'do! How did he forget the name of the famous Bhakhti saint-ChaitanyiaMahaprabhu and his contribution to Bengali Culture and to the overall Indian culture?Sen's views on population control for India are equally marvelous/ridiculous. He wants us to do nothing about it now; just wait! The population bomb will defuse itself automatically, he has calculated. He also derides China's one child policy that saved it from an abyss.Above all it prevented that demographic imbalance which threatens Gandhi-Nehru India with another partition sooner or later. Just his American Govt.'s view and long term planning! Senility?

The above draws my attention to another sect of comical luminaries; called Historians.In these commercial times when anything can be for sale these intellectuals have proved no exception.And such people with an agenda or a distorted view of life or towards a community, group or nation can sabotage,and cut the veryvery roots of truth. They often seem not to understand what they themselves write.Nehru,for example,has written a book on world history but failed to remember how Greece and Turkey peacefully exchanged 1.5 million of their populations in 1923,twenty four years before the Indian partition which claimed about the same 1.5 million lives.Who is responsible?Who is responsible for the continuous blood shed that occurs in communal clashes in India, ever since then?Why don't communal wars occur in Pakistan,Turkey or Greece?Was Jinnah a more practical and a wise politician? Who on Indian side, agreed to that partition and what did India gain from it? Premiership for Nehru? Read him praising the Chinese, for their peaceful and highly mature cultured life and thought and one gathers that he only copied, never understood History. As a result he proved a failure in peace as well a failure in war. He failed his nation at every crucial juncture. His economic model which was a hoch-poch of soviet system and the traditional bania (capitalist) method had to be thrown out by his own party. Similarly, another well-known 'historian' Romilla Thappar, with her eyes closed to scientific reasoning and even ordinary common sense, in her book, borrows a full page of some unnamed unknown Afghan 'historian' to declare that the huge 'linga' weighing several tons at Somnath temple was suspended in air with the magnetic attraction of load stones lying in the roof of the then temple in AD.1010 when Mahmood gazni invaded and destroyed that. Was the science and calculation of electromagnetic forces so developed in India then? Can ISRO or NASA perform such a miracle even today? Examples can be multiplied but it should suffice to name a world-famous historian named Gibbon who, swayed in his praise of ancient Roman achievements, categorically declares that the happiest and the most prosperous period for all humanity has been the time when Augustus (Octavius) ruled Rome. Judge for your-selves please!

It may not be very foolish to say that writing a great book on history is perhaps not a very difficult task. One should know well the art of copying for this. In writing a book of history one has only to selectively copy what has already been written by others; no originality or research is obviously needed. Some change of language and an occasional emphasis does the trick. And one earns the qualification of being a great Historian for free.

Back again, please remember that in later years and old age, one's needs and hence expenses are automatically reduced to a small fraction of that of one's earlier years. Same applies to expenses of any serious/ terminal illness in that epoch of life. There is a limit to what doctors can do for you. Don't become a prey to false hopes given by them. They have their own compulsions of meeting the expenses of their establishments, of providing for fat profits for owners of large hospitals, and their personal standing in modern days. Basic treatment for maintenance of life is not very costly. Please avoid prolonged hospitalization. A hospital bed plus an oxygen cylinder in the patient's own bed room and if needed a semiskilled nurse, plus regular home visits by a physician will cost a fraction of a modern hospital bill and is very consoling and reassuring to an aged patient. Ask for avoidance of unnecessary investigation and tests.

Summary {this is to repeat my words that gold is found in sand and diamonds among stones and pebbles and that this world is full of invaluable delights. It is just a matter of one's inclination and a little effort to reach them. Accordingly, we stress development of a scientific temper and a finer poetic temperament for better discernment of reality. Let us remember that fairs, festivities and feasts of life will never end nor its turbulence. In any case, life is getting more interesting by the day. Only we will not be here all the time. So, let us make the most and the best of it. Plan it? No Sir.

People forget their plans and new-year and birthday promises just the next morning. So, what can happen to your lengthy plan covering a whole life? Simply try to change your thinking on some subjects like your own importance in your life, the place of love in life, how much money and how many bungalows and how many wardrobes full of garments etc. does one need to live reasonably well. This is not to advocate renunciation of pleasures or to become a sadhu or hermit. On the other hand it is a recommendation for full enjoyment minus too much material greed. Some amount of greed is necessary to go about in life but let us have limits. Its excess ultimately leads to tears in one's own eyes and heart burn in others, one day. We advocate that life be lived and enjoyed full size but without tears. We are not against any one's riches but one must keep his outlook on life alive during life's struggles. Let us live out life on our own terms and not on the dictates or directions of others or of this schizophrenic society. Don't forget to look at and celebrate nature's gifts, the beauty of life itself. The fleeting but mesmerizing visions of flowery girls, the living loving meadows and mountains, the singing streams the beauty of a cultivated garden as also of the forlorn desert and wilderness with their "shunya"- the beauty invites nothingness the beauty of my civilized humane leopard and many many countless blessings They cannot be neglected. Their delights are invaluable.

Once you realize the worth of nature's blessings, your perspective about man-made acquisitions and glamours will automatically change. Now you can strike the right balance between the two and that is what is needed. Combine your reasonably measured earthly acquisitions with nature's bounties and you will be a happier person. If one can live smiling and laughing why not then? That is the submission.

Swayed by the abounding delights of nature all around us **we have neglected to talk about man's own creations of no less value and worth**. I am talking about our achievements in arts and literature. Unfortunately, my own acquaintance with these has been extremely little but have judged their value, so to say, from a distance. Even so I do admit that the slightest contact with or exposure to these is enough to change one's course of life and banish its sterility if there be.

Read king Lear, for example, and you know how to fight back injustice, tyranny and treachery breach of trust worse when that comes from one's own flesh and blood. It is not a story but a principle of living that is enunciated and told in words that awaken one's soul. 'I am more sinned against than sinning, hmm' must shake the Gods, if any be, out of their slumber towards what wrongs are perpetrated in their created world. Every word enthuses and every sentence penetrates to awaken one's dormant being and conscience. It is a song for rebellion told in burning words. Hmm.

It gives strength to withstand wrongs!

Searching for a meaning to life or its purpose, dwell for a moment on Hamlet's soliloquy 'To be or not be'. Introspect and reflect, you are near your goal. Consider "Rest is all silence" And you are nearer. Now take up my Ghalib, understand it. It, like Keats, sings of love, beauty and truth. (Sat,ChitAnand),Lo, your riddles are solved!

What better than this companionship especially in one's retirement. One's joy stands assured.

I am not in any position by dint of ignorance, to talk about other great works but these must be equally invigorating, I believe. Same ignorance prevents me from talking about other arts in particular about music but from a distance can feel that they represent the very essence of life, no less its charm.

Right thinking in the long run turns into right habits and these in turn give one a right way. It is a gradual process and takes its time. This life in itself is a process-a work in progress on the shoulders of our physical body which is the scaffolding on which life rests. It is rightly said that our eyes cannot see what the mind doesn't know and vice-versa. Put a sketch of habits before it, including the habit of an easy smile on face (as stated in the beginning) it will incorporate that into itself and the result is a peaceful, happy time for you. It is a matter of gradual practice (Abhyas). Instead of asking for help or forgiveness for sins from skies, try to do what you need to do yourself. That cultivates self-confidence and a spirit of independence:' Place a sketch of optimism, self-help and self-confidence before your mind. Gradually our eyes will see light, love and laughter dawning and it is a life, different. Remember the famed Persian Muslim poet Hafiz where he says that a man's misfortune prevents him from realizing that he is the Lord himself but has assumed the role of a beggar seeking help from others asalms. This translates into: Ahambrahmosmi",Please realize that. Do what you think is right and what keeps you happy. Nothing good or bad but thinking makes it so. In the process please don't forget the innocent days of your adolescence and youth. They were truly pleasant for everyone, poor as well as the rich, religious or otherwise. These are the days of most men's upward as well as uphill journey in life. These impart modesty of behavior and moderation of thought in later life. Most people start small in life so better that we don't feign having come up with a silver spoon in our mouth. Please have consideration for the poor and those below you.

A famous couplet, by a renowned Islamic scholar Allama Iqbal almost sums up what we have said earlier.

"khudi (meaning self or Aham-a Sanskrit word) kokarbuland"-----meaning 'train your 'self' or elevate your 'self, en-noble it' to live a likeable, respectable (pleasurable)life. Iqbal who is held in high esteem by all, also recognizes the importance of cultivating the self(Aham).He emphasizes the importance of 'KHUDI' for uplifting one-self. Who has after all seen God? It could be a hypothetical supposition as well, not even a reasonable inference. So trust in self. "I can, you also can" should be the Mantra of life. In any case our submission is that a happier state of mind is a very easy thing to achieve. Simply learn to love and it is all pleasure there-after. I am not talking of conjugal love only. Universe of love is very vast and conjugal love though fundamentally important forms just a small fraction of it. No grievances, grudges or animosities of past to disturb. Forgive and forget. If it is difficult to forgive because you feel grossly harmed or hurt by someone then simply forget him, tear off the page that bears his name and account in your mental diary. I do it in my life and have often succeeded in maintaining my peace of mind in dire situations.

About 'Love' there are some meaningful words/advice given in 'Upanishad' either in katha or Issoa Upanishad, I don't exactly remember; These state, 'O wife your husband does not love you for your sake but for his own and vice versa; O father the son does not love you for your sake but for his own' and vice versa and so on with the entire cluster of human relations. And this is exactly corroborated by psychoanalysis and modern scientific thought. But such selfish thinking even when 100% true, will not be acceptable to any one in life. If for example a lover tells his beloved that he loves her only to please himself from her company, she will forthwith spurn him as a greedy selfish and a mannerless brute. So the mental mechanisms as described by Freud come into play and the man totally denies his personal interest in the process. He on the other, through an unconscious process inverses his desire claiming that he lays himself completely at her behest and can readily give even his life for her, because she is too lovable and too good. He swears that his love for her is pure and selfless and that he cannot live without her. This naturally pleases the beloved and she too by the same unconscious process of 'inversion' feels and declares identical altruist and immortal love for him. And that is what forms our day-to-day world of love and observable affection. So, saying I don't say that all professions of love in the world are untrue but we do recognize that all parties concerned play the game for the sake of their own need and nobody has time nor need to analyze another's words and vows of eternal faithfulness. Everyone has the same compulsions. It is a universal happening and hence accepted as 'Pious' love' without any doubt. Shockingly this pious love is all founded on base desires of self-benefit and self-love only. It is all self-centered pleasure and benefits. Alas, this world is woven out of 'Moon beams' as described by Somerset Maugham. Remembering these facts helps one to be realistic and not demand too much of life, that is the message. Human desires and greed have to have limits. And when greed is reduced happiness enters. Gani Kashmiri, the poet, as already said, was a happy man calling himself a lion and the master of untold riches because he had won over greed. He was realistic to the core and so enjoyed his life like a king.

At some railway platforms we often find a slogan written 'Travel light'; don't carry too much baggage. This is wise. It makes for a carefree journey; it is a pleasant experience if one travels with the least baggage. Exactly the same applies to one's life. Life also is a long journey, the lesser baggage and junk you collect and carry on your head in this journey the more carefree you remain and the more pleasant the travel will be. This applies to both rich and the poor equally. In fact life at extremes is usually not a happy one. Rich people are as troubled as are the very poor. It is the middle socioeconomic class that are the least unhappy in life. Benefits of moderation and modesty!

Nevertheless, anyone can go on collecting whatever pleases him. Only don't carry your riches *on* your head. It is desirable to cultivate an attitude of detachment. It automatically gives pleasure. One feels light and free, as if relieved of a weight. Ultimately he is the richest man on earth who declares himself a satisfied person. He has less worries!

But overall learn to laugh, please. At least please laugh at the web of illusion that is woven around us which we take so seriously and then strut and fret our hour on the stage of life and then are gone. Somerset Maugham says our world is made of 'Moon-beams'; it is illusory (Mayavi),but like our wise-man Nehru, we delight in imagining that the world will collapse in our absence. The occasion deserves loud laughter. Even artificial laughter is not out of place and it helps; it makes others laugh, at least on seeing you smile and laugh at everything. Their laughter will react on you and evoke genuine laughter and pleasure in you also. Also please laugh at your own follies in life. Sportsmanly accepting one's own deficiencies and faults is a sign of mental normalcy. No special effort is needed. Keep the objective in view; its basic principles will in time permeate the whole personality. It happens automatically though gradually.

Kindly note that I have said and even preached many
and varied things above and it will appear that I must be
a very good and perfect and accomplished person
myself. Far from that, sirs. But I am trying my best in
the hope that 'I can. And I am sure so can you'. Please
try.

END...

Books by same author:
1. 'Leaking secrets', of doctor's ways and practice
2. 'Musing of a psychiatrist' random thoughts.